SUBJECT GUIDE
TO HUMOR:

Anecdotes, Facetiae and Satire
from 365 Periodicals, 1968-74

by

Jean Spealman Kujoth

The Scarecrow Press, Inc.
Metuchen, N.J.   1976

Library of Congress Cataloging in Publication Data

Kujoth, Jean Spealman.
    Subject guide to humor.

    Includes index.
    1. Wit and humor--Indexes. I. Title.
Z6514.W5K84   [PN6147]   016.80887   76-4865
ISBN 0-8108-0924-9

To

R. K.

CONTENTS

INTRODUCTION

This guide lists by general subject field, specific subject, author, and title, over 1,800 humorous, anecdotal, and satiric articles and stories published in 365 periodicals from 1968 through 1974.

The reader may here locate items for personal enjoyment or for use in speech writing, group discussions, etc. The classified section of the book presents the pieces and their sources in author sequence under each of fifteen general subject fields. The other three sections refer to the pieces by subject-field prefix letter and article number.

Periodical indexes consulted include the Air University Index to Military Periodicals; Art Index; Biological and Agricultural Index; Business Periodicals Index; Cumulative Index to Nursing Literature; Education Index; Humanities Index; Index Medicus; Index to Legal Periodicals; Library Literature; Music Index; Popular Periodical Index; Readers' Guide to Periodical Literature; and Social Sciences and Humanities Index.

CLASSIFIED SECTION

ART, ARCHITECTURE, AND DESIGN

A1   Ace, Goodman. "Skirting the Question, and Vice Versa." Saturday Review 52:4, 2/8/69.

A2   Bernstein, Leonard S. "How Much Is That Painting in the Window?" House Beautiful 113:38+, 11/71.

A3   Blum, Sam. "Oh! Fashion! One Man's Look at the Preening of America." Redbook 136:79+, 4/71.

A4   Bombeck, Erma. "Fashion Follies." Good Housekeeping 177:58+, 9/73.

A5   ———. "Me and the Miniskirt." Good Housekeeping 169:58+, 9/69.

A6   Brogan, Denis William. "Myth America." Antiquity 42:17-19, 3/68.

A7   Butlin, Martin. "Eighteenth Century Art Scandal: Nathaniel Hone's 'The Conjuror'." Connoisseur 174: 1-9, 5/70.

A8   Clapham, R. C. "A Planner, as Seen by the Public; a Planner as Seen by a Planner." Town Planning Institute Journal 56:403, 11/70.

A9   Corcoran, Paul A. "Amazing Maze." Theology Today 30:407-8, 1/74.

A10   Finkelstein, Irving L. and Kibbey, Richard. "Quotations from Student Papers." Art Journal 31 no. 3: 240, Winter 1971-72.

A11   Gescheidt, Alfred. "Pro's Secrets." Popular Photography 68:102-5+, 2/71.

A12   Guilfoyle, J. Roger. Editorial: "The Future of Design Is in Your Hands." Industrial Design 17:29, 4/70.

A13   Hart, Sir William. "General Ruminations." Town and Country Planning 38:164, 3/70.

A14   Hess, Thomas B. "Art Comics of Ad Reinhardt." Artforum 12:46-51, 4/74.

A15   Jencks, Charles. "Pigeon-holing Made Difficult: Diagram Showing the Relation of One Architect to Another Based on Historical Influence." Architectural Design 39:582, 11/69.

A16   Jensen, Oliver. "Letter from the Editor." American

       Heritage 23:2, 8/72.

A17 Johnson, Ray. "Abandoned Chickens." <u>Art in America</u>
       62:107-12, 11/74.

A18 Johnston, Robert P. "Quotations from Student Examina-
       tion Papers." <u>Art Journal</u> 30 no. 4:382, Summer
       1971; reply, A. S. Harris, 31 no. 3:366, Spring 1972.

A19 Jones, Becky. "Confessions of a Camera Nut." <u>Seven-</u>
       <u>teen</u> 33:80+, 5/74.

       Kaiserman, David. SEE: Shepley, Christopher.

       Kibbey, Richard. SEE: Finkelstein, Irving L.

A20 Look. "Look Invites You to Play the City Game."
       <u>Look</u> 32:104-5, 6/11/68.

A21 Magee, Mae. "Giving My All for Art: Building a Prop
       Boat." <u>Good Housekeeping</u> 179:52+, 10/74.

A22 Mannes, Marc. "Who Has the Last Laugh?" <u>Historic</u>
       <u>Preservation</u> 25:18-19, 10/73.

A23 Mutrux, Robert H. "Final Presentation: Athens in the
       Year of the Eighty-second Olympiad 447 B.C." <u>Pro-</u>
       <u>gressive Architecture</u> 51:108-9, 9/70.

A24 Nathan, Simon. "Simon Says: Bunab Model No. 7."
       <u>Modern Photography</u> 32:44+, 5/68.

A25 Nemser, Cindy. "Interview with an Anonymous Artist."
       <u>Art Education</u> 23:32-5, 1/70.

A26 Peck, Richard. "Future-Laugh." <u>Saturday Review</u> 55:
       69-70, 8/26/72.

A27 Peterson, Charles E. "Use of Architects in America,
       1834." <u>Antiques</u> 100:876, 12/71.

A28 Polk, George Merritt, Jr. "From the General to the
       Practitioner." <u>AIA Journal</u> 50:82, 8/68.

A29 Raleigh, Henry P. "Cool Platonism or the Hipster's
       Heraclitus; an Undated Dialogue." <u>Art Journal</u> 28
       no. 4:375+, Summer 1969.

A30 Rea, Marjorie. "How to Behave in an Artist's Studio,
       1877." <u>Antiques</u> 100:868, 12/71.

A31 Robbins, Jhan. "Of Miniskirts and Pantyhose." <u>Read-</u>
       <u>er's Digest</u> 96:81-3, 3/70.

A32 Rohdenburg, Ernest. "Misreported Quidor Court Case."
       <u>American Art Journal</u> 2 no. 1:74-80, Spring 1970.

A33 Ross, Simon. "Monkey Business; Planning Competition
       for a Building for Breeding Monkeys." <u>Town and</u>
       <u>Country Planning</u> 39:514, 11/71.

A34 _____. Personal Column: "Christmas Spirit or
       Under the Influence." <u>Town and Country Planning</u>
       39:562-3, 12/71.

A35 Shepley, Christopher and Kaiserman, David. "Grotton
       Reorganized--the First 100 Days." <u>Planner</u> 60:792-
       4, 7/74.

A36   Sheppard, Eugenia. "Are You Slightly Rectangular?"
        Harper's Bazaar 102:238-9, 10/69.

A37   . "Bodies Are So Boring." Harper's Bazaar
        102:168, 4/69.

A38   . "I Really Will." Harper's Bazaar 102:133,
        1/69.

A39   Smart, James. "British Aristocrat Turns Developer,
        Plans New City in Under-developed Country." Town
        and Country Planning 37:525-6, 11/69.

A40   Spade, Rupert. "Semantic Drunkenness." Architectural
        Design 39:124, 3/69.

A41   Stanton, Will. "Grand What? and Other Great Works
        of Earth Art." Atlantic Monthly 231:95-7, 6/73.

A42   Stephens, Suzanne. "W.T.C. 2023 (Originally the
        World Trade Center)." Architectural Forum 138:
        56-61, 4/73.

A43   Stevenson, James. "Notes from an Exhibition." New
        Yorker 45:32-3, 3/22/69.

A44   Vasari, pseud. "Buying Van Goghs for a Song and Oth-
        er Stories." Art News 71:12+, 10/72.

A45   . "Vasari Diary: Mysterious Monet and Other
        Stories." Art News 72:12-13, 11/73.

A46   Vestal, David. "How to Be a Photographic Snob."
        Popular Photography 73:104-5+, 8/73.

A47   Wagner, Geoffrey. "Plato on Pop Art." National Re-
        view 22:1066-7, 10/6/70.

A48   Wendell, Lehman. "Looking Back at Ninety." U.S.
        Camera and Travel 31:22+, 6/68.

A49   Wheeler, Kenneth D. "Architectural Prayer--Of Sorts."
        AIA Journal 56:59, 11/71.

A50   Williamson, Dereck. "Shutter Shudders." Saturday
        Review 53:4, 12/5/70.

ECONOMICS AND BUSINESS

B1   Ace, Goodman.   "Chic Sheikh."   Saturday Review World
     1:8, 3/23/74.

B2   _____.   "Deficit Saving."   Saturday Review World 1:
     10, 7/27/74.

B3   _____.   "High Diddle Diddle."   Saturday Review
     World 1:34, 2/23/74.

B4   _____.   "Incommunicado."   Saturday Review World
     1:34, 6/15/74.

B5   _____.   "One Man's Loan Is Another Man's Lien."
     Saturday Review World 1:10, 10/23/73.

B6   _____.   "Puny Express."   Saturday Review 52:6,
     3/29/69.

B7   _____.   "Witness for the Defense."   Saturday Re-
     view World 1:33, 3/9/74.

B8   Baker, Russell.   "Bundling Power."   New York Times
     Magazine p. 5, 1/27/74.

B9   _____.   "Chaste Deduction; Tax on Sex."   New York
     Times Magazine p. 6, 4/15/74.

B10 _____.   "Conglomeration of Newt Ogilvy."   Life 66:
     4, 4/18/69.

B11 _____.   "Crisis Crisis."   New York Times Maga-
     zine p. 6, 1/20/74.

B12 _____.   "Fine Print."   New York Times Magazine
     p. 6, 12/2/73.

B13 _____.   "More Fine Print."   New York Times Mag-
     azine p. 6, 1/6/74.

B14 _____.   "Passing the Books."   New York Times
     Magazine p. 6, 6/2/74.

B15 _____.   "Taxburg Address."   New York Times Mag-
     azine p. 6, 4/15/73.

B16 _____.   "Work Fanatics; Work Habits of White
     House Staff Members."   New York Times Magazine
     p. 4, 8/19/73.

B17 Bayliss, William H.   "Management by CSROEPM."

Harvard Business Review 47:85-9, 3/69.

B18   Berger, Mike. "Management by Results; Planning the Battle of Jericho." Dun's 100:111+, 11/72.

B19   Bernstein, Leonard S. "How to Discriminate in Hiring." Dun's 100:105+, 10/72.

B20   _____. "How to Make a Million Dollars on Your Vacation; Rain Free Insurance." Holiday 49:26-7, 7/71.

B21   Blackburn, Sara. "Taxi!" New Yorker 44:102-4, 2/8/69.

B22   Bombeck, Erma. "My Checkbook and Me." Good Housekeeping 170:64+, 3/70.

B23   _____. "Tax Time at Our House." Good Housekeeping 176:76+, 3/73.

B24   Brien, Alan. "Hard Times." New Statesman 76:200, 8/16/68.

B25   Brown, Bob. Editorial: "Effect of the Bureaucracy on Automobiles." Car and Driver 19:6, 5/74.

B26   Brutus, pseud. "Confessions of a Stockbroker." Atlantic Monthly 228:46-52, 7/71.

B27   Buchwald, Art. "Washington Householder Speaks His Mind; Interview." House and Garden 138:26+, August 1970.

B28   _____. "Where Are They Now?" Saturday Evening Post 243:32, Summer 1971.

B29   Buckwalter, Len. "Five Worst Jobs." Mechanix Illustrated 66:54-6+, 10/70.

B30   Burgess, Anthony, pseud. "Just $10, Please, for My Mugger." Vogue 161:112, 1/73.

B31   Capp, Al. "Why I Am Not Rich." Saturday Evening Post 246:48, 3/74.

B32   Christian Century. "Fine Art of Fund-Raising." Christian Century 86:729, 5/21/69.

B33   Cochran, Betsy. "Open Letter to CU." Consumer Reports 33:500, 9/68.

B34   Collier, Barnard Law. "Grassing of America." Saturday Review 55:12-4, 7/29/72.

B35   Conger, Lesley. "Note from My Real Office." Writer 83:9-10, 10/70.

B36   Cotler, Gordon. "Fast Food for Thought." New Yorker 50:39, 10/7/74.

B37   _____. "Using 1957-59 as a Base, Try Stealing Home." New Yorker 46:26-7, 5/16/70.

B38   Cratchit, Bob, pseud. "How to Cheat on Your Income Tax: a Guide." Ramparts 10:32-3+, 4/72.

B39   Culliton, James William. "Once upon a Seesaw." Harvard Business Review 52:99-109, 3/74.

B40   Dana, Roger W. "Forum." Dun's 97:113, 5/71.

B41   D'Angelo, Lou. "For a Limited Time Only." Satur-
      day Review 55:86, 6/17/72.

B42   Dible, Donald M. "Case against Gargantuan, Inc."
      Dun's 100:85-6, 9/72.

B43   Drubdovi, Andy. "Fold! Spingle! Mutilate!" National
      Review 23:1252, 11/5/71.

B44   Dun's. "How Do You Face the Annual Meeting?"
      Dun's 95:48-9+, 4/70.

B45   _____. "Wry Report on Annual Reports." Dun's
      95:32-3, 5/70.

B46   Elliott, Bob and Goulding, Ray. "Aerospace Bonus
      Boys." Atlantic Monthly 221:52-6, 6/68.

B47   Esquire. "Take Them They're Yours; Six Jobs in
      Search of the (Truly) Liberated Woman." Esquire
      73:63-8, 2/70.

B48   Farnsworth, Clyde. "Letter from Paris." Saturday
      Review World 1:28, 1/26/74.

B49   Fettig, Art. "What on Earth Did You Bid on That For?"
      Farm Journal 93:30C, 6/69.

B50   Finn, Chester E., Jr. "Ph.D. as Piglet." National
      Review 24:588, 5/26/72.

B51   Flavin, George. "Sam Snodgrass Rides Again; Over-
      supply of Ph.D.'s." America 124:406-7, 4/17/71.

B52   Forbes. "Sex and the Energy Crisis." Forbes. 112:
      27, 12/1/73.

B53   Gans, Herbert J. "Tale of Princes and Paupers."
      Current 93:62-4, 3/68.

B54   Gittelson, Natalie. "Too Rich and Too Thin." Harper's
      Bazaar 102:19+, 8/69.

B55   Gleiser, Molly. "Obsolescent Life." Harper's 249:
      68-70, 9/74.

      Goulding, Ray. SEE: Elliott, Bob.

B56   Granholm, Jackson W. "Case for Negative Money."
      National Review 24:102, 2/4/72.

B57   Greenleaf, Warren T. "Are You Getting Your Share?
      An Open Letter to American Educators." Phi Delta
      Kappan 50:inside back cover, 10/68.

B58   Halliday, E. M. "Short Primer of Style." Horizon 10:
      120, Summer 1968.

B59   Hayne, Arnold. "Supply and Demand." Look 34:92,
      12/15/70.

B60   Jarman, Rufus. "Grandpa and the Wolves of Wall
      Street." Saturday Evening Post 244:76-7+, Spring
      1972.

B61   Joel, Helmuth W., Jr. "Doing It with 1040!" Saturday
      Review 55:6, 3/18/72.

B62   Keefauver, John. "Two Post Office Departments To-
        day!" National Review 23:199, 2/23/71.
B63   Keillor, Garrison. "People's Shopper." New Yorker
        49:37-9, 2/24/73.
B64   Kelley, Douglas Ward. "Dig It." Mademoiselle 77:
        234, 5/73.
B65   Leeds, Morton. "People and Products: a Useful Deca-
        logue." Vital Speeches 36:303-6, 3/1/70.
B66   Life. "Panic in a Pear Tree; Cost of the Twelve Days
        of Christmas Presents." Life 73:112, 12/15/72.
B67   Lipez, Richard. "Home Buyers' Guide." Harper's
        247:112, 11/73.
B68   _____. "Inflation Made Easy." Progressive 38:66,
        10/74.
B69   _____. "WINners." Progressive 38:66, 12/74.
B70   Logsdon, Gene. "Real Food Price Villain." Farm
        Journal 96:A3, 8/72.
B71   _____. "You Could Make a Fortune in the Problem
        Business." Farm Journal 94:40-1+, 3/70.
B72   _____. "You're in Show Business." Farm Journal
        97:12-13, 6/73.
B73   _____. "You're Not Just a Farmer, You're in Show
        Business!" Farm Journal 97:30-A3, 10/73.
B74   Longwell, Maude. "In the Go-Go Summertime." Farm
        Journal 93:36-7, 8/69.
B75   Louviere, Vernon. "Save Enough Fuel? It's Child's
        Play." Nation's Business 62:36, 9/74.
B76   Mano, D. Keith. "Burials; High-rise Mausoleum."
        National Review 25:896-7, 8/17/73.
B77   McSherry, Mary. "My Short and Secret Life as a
        Cleaning Woman." McCall's 97:78-9+, 10/69.
B78   Mead, Shepherd. "How to Succeed in Business Abroad
        Without Really Trying." Saturday Evening Post 243:
        82-4+, Summer; 90-2+, Fall 1971.
B79   Mercker, Frances. "My Mother, the Investor."
        Changing Times 26:6, 6/72.
B80   Millengen, John Gideon. "Archaic Bellyaches about
        Doctors' Fees"; excerpt from Curiosities of Medical
        Experience. Today's Health 48:32-4, 8/70.
B81   Morgan, Henry. "Mr. Sullivan Discusses the Stock
        Market (with Apologies to Mr. Arbuthnot)." Satur-
        day Review 54:4, 1/23/71.
B82   National Review. "First Ninety Days." National Re-
        view 24:344-5, 3/31/72.
B83   New Republic. TRB from Washington: "As Seen from
        Space; Trimming Food Stamp Benefits." New Re-
        public 171:4, 12/14/74.

B84 New Yorker. "Jersey Ritual: Annual Meeting of Hess
      Oil and Chemical Corporation; Letter from Anthro-
      pologist." New Yorker 45:30-1, 5/31/69.
B85 Newsweek. "Devil's Advocate." Newsweek 79:84+,
      3/27/72.
B86 Noonan, Joseph. "Whither Advertising?" Catholic
      World 209:126-8, 6/69.
B87 North, Gary. "Modest Macro-Economic Proposal."
      National Review 24:1353, 12/8/72.
B88 Novick, Sheldon. "Jaundiced Eye." Environment 16:
      inside cover, 5/74.
B89 Pfizer, Beryl. "End of a Beautiful Friendship with
      My Friendly Bank." McCall's 96:92-3, 3/69.
B90 Phillips, J. N. "Where Are You Miss Bailiwick?"
      Saturday Evening Post 243:60-2+, Fall 1971.
B91 Reed, J. D. "In a Happy Hunting Ground: Ordering
      Sporting Goods." Sports Illustrated 37:48-50+, 12/
      11/72.
B92 Reiss, Alvin H. "Who Remembers M.A.M.A.?"
      Esquire 71:162-3, 3/69.
B93 Riccardo, David, pseud. "Great 1970 Market Crash."
      Esquire 72:50+, 12/69.
B94 Rickenbacker, William F. "Christmas Greetings from
      the Dismal Science." National Review 25:33, 1/5/
      73.
B95 Russell, Mark. "Quips that Are Making Washington
      Laugh." Nation's Business 62:36-8, 12/74.
B96 Sales Management. "Stop Me If You Heard This One
      Before." Sales Management 110:13-14, 5/28/73.
B97 Schoenstein, Ralph. "Day America Went Bananas;
      Reaction to Shortages." Today's Health 62:42-3+,
      5/74.
B98 _____. "Trying to Ketchup to a Hamburger You
      Can Relish." Today's Health 50:26-9, 10/72.
B99 Schrader, Steven. "Good Times in the Garden of
      Eden." Harper's 247:5, 7/73.
B100 Shepherd, Jean. Column. Car and Driver 20:15-19,
      9/74.
B101 Smith, Adam, pseud. "If Something Happens to Me,
      Whatever You Do, Don't Sell My IBM"; excerpts
      from The Money Game. Atlantic Monthly 221:54-8,
      4/68.
B102 Stanton, Will. "How Can You Lose a Swimming Pool?"
      Reader's Digest 92:88-90, 4/68.
B103 _____. "Open Season." Saturday Review 52:4,
      1/18/69; Reader's Digest 94:81-3, 3/69.
B104 Strout, Richard L. "Why We Need the Poor." New

Republic 169:14-15, 11/17/73.
B105 Sutherland, Don. "Birth of a Salesman." Travel and
     Camera 32:78-9+, 4/69.
B106 Swinnerton, A. R. "My Downtown Office." Retirement
     Living 13:36-7, 8/73.
B107 Tracy, Lane. "Postscript to the Peter Principle."
     Harvard Business Review 50:65-71, 7/72; reply with
     rejoinder, R. W. Smuts, 50:158+, 9/72.
B108 Vaughan, Bill. "This Is a Recording"; excerpts from
     Half the Battle. Reader's Digest 93:81-2, 8/68.
B109 Weisse, Edward B. and Zalas, Benjamin. "Student De-
     mands; Cybernetic City Cringes." Clearing House
     46:309-11, 1/72.
B110 Weith, Warren. Column. Car and Driver 19:22+,
     4/74.
B111 Williamson, Dereck. "Blotching the Job." Saturday
     Review 55:71, 7/1/72.
B112 _____. "They've Got Your Number, and Theirs,
     Too." Saturday Review 51:2+, 4/13/68; Reader's
     Digest 93:49-51, 7/68.
     Zalas, Benjamin. SEE: Weisse, Edward B.
B113 Zinsser, William Knowlton. "Annual Meeting of the
     Corporation." New York Times Magazine p.9+, 5/
     16/71.
B114 _____. "Annual Report of the National Refractory
     and Brake Company." Life 66:59-60+, 2/28/69.
B115 _____. "Check and Supercheck." Life 71:14, 10/
     22/71.
B116 _____. "Everything You Didn't Want to Know about
     Phase 2." Life 71:56A+, 11/19/71.
B117 _____. "Frankly, Miss Dodds." Atlantic Monthly
     231:94-6, 4/73.
B118 _____. "Have a Swell July." Life 72:16, 6/30/72.
B119 _____. "Zip Code Caper." Life 64:12, 2/23/68.

EDUCATION

C1 Ace, Goodman. "Two Thoughts of School." Saturday
    Review 53:4, 11/28/70.
C2 Adams, Carolyn H. "Emperor's Fish." Today's Edu-
    cation 60:29, 4/71.
C3 Aikman, Arthur. "On the Education Expert." Phi
    Delta Kappan 54:549, 4/73.
C4 Allen, Don and Taylor, Halsey. "Adventures in Edu-
    cation at Herbert Hoover High." Media and Meth-
    ods 8:39, 11/71; 30-1, 12/71; 37-8, 2/72; 31-8,
    3/72; 33-4, 4/72; 27-9, 5/72; 9:40-1, 9/72; 40-1,
    11/72; 41, 12/72; 44-5, 1/73; 79, 2/73; 57, 4/73;
    10:52, 11/73; 24-5, 12/73.
C5 Allen, Melvyn R. "Between the Times." Today's Ed-
    ucation 61:36, 10/72.
C6 Amidei, Mary Kay. "I Made It for You!" Instructor
    80:159-60, 8/70.
C7 Anthony, Albert S. "Some Unprinciples for Successful
    Innovation." Education Digest 37:32-3, 11/71.
C8 _____. "Twenty Unprinciples for Successful Innova-
    tion." Clearing House 46:32-4, 9/71.
C9 Arons, Arnold. "Educational Practices: an Expert
    View of Current Trends." Physics Teacher 11:487-
    8, 11/73; reply, Judith D. Aubrecht, 12:233-4, 4/74.
C10 Avner, R. A. "How to Produce Ineffective CAI Mater-
    ial." Educational Technology 14:26-7, 8/74.
C11 Bachrach, Beatrice. "Remember." School and Com-
    munity 60:12-13, 1/74.
C12 Baker, Russell. "Excellence of Welby Stitch, Jr."
    Life 66:24, 3/21/69.
C13 Behrens, Laurence. "Stratford Papers." College Eng-
    lish 35:422-6+, 1/74.
C14 Benjamin, James M. "Bonus Plan: an Innovation for
    Quality." Clearing House 46:336-8, 2/72.
C15 Berman, Maxine. "Teachers at Bat." Saturday Re-

view Education 1:11-12, 3/73.

C16 Blair, Harold Lynn. "Alfred's Northern Lights."
     School and Community 60:35, 3/74.

C17 Bonner, Thomas N. "Modest Proposal Speaks for It-
     self." Compact 7:36-7, 5/73.

C18 Boren, James H. "Making the World Safe for Bureauc-
     racy." NASSP Bulletin 57:19-23, 5/73; Education
     Digest 39:36-8, 10/73.

C19 Boyles, Beatrice C. "Public Spirited Principal; How
     to Become One." National Elementary Principal
     49:31-2, 5/70.

C20 Bozzone, August. "Signs of the Times: Introducing
     Placard Writing in the Curriculum." New York
     State Education 58:25, 5/71.

C21 Brennan, John. "Jimmy Breathless Goes to College."
     National Review 22:258, 3/10/70.

C22 Briggs, Ken. "How Not to Become a Well-Paid Educa-
     tional Consultant." Journal of Teacher Education
     25:80, Spring 1974.

C23 Brodinsky, Ben. "Wonderland of Innovations." Phi
     Delta Kappan 58:back cover, 11/74.

C24 Brody, Steve. "Hold That Line!" Today's Education
     62:29, 11/73.

C25 _____. "Rose Ann Lee by Any Other Name." To-
     day's Education 63:65, 3/74.

C26 _____. "Sitting Pretty." Today's Education 62:29-
     30, 9/73.

C27 _____. "Sound Reasoning." Today's Education 63:
     93: 1/74.

C28 Buchwald, Art. "All Protests Met at Goodcheer U."
     Today's Education 57:25, 9/68.

C29 Burns, Richard and Harrell, Roger L. "Game of One
     Downsmanship or One Upsmanship Down." Clearing
     House 46:96-7, 10/71.

C30 Buroker, Geets. "Doing Your Own Thing." Instructor
     82:16-18, 3/73.

C31 Calisch, Richard. "Don't Talk, Communicate!" Eng-
     lish Journal 62:1010-11, 10/73.

C32 Canfield, Roger B. "Monkey Movement." National Re-
     view 24:417, 4/14/72.

C33 Caplan, Richard M. "Built-In Orderly Organized
     Knowledge System." Journal of the Iowa Medical So-
     ciety 63:404, 8/73.

C34 Carr, John C. "Cliches for the '70's." Clearing
     House 47:185-6, 11/72.

C35 Chamberlain, John. "Tale of Two Dropouts." NEA
     Journal 57:54, 5/68.

C36   Chandler, W. Porter III, pseud. "Lot of Learning Is
       a Dangerous Thing." Harvard Business Review 50:
       122-31, 3/72; reply P. R. Chandler, 50:30-2, 7/72.
C37   Clark, John R. "College Progress." College English
       32:691-5, 3/71.
C38   _____. "Faculties at Large (the Campus Citizenship
       Papers)." College English 33:571-7, 2/72.
C39   Clark, Sharon. "In the Name of Education; the Play's
       the Thing: Drama." Clearing House 48:311-16, 1/7
C40   Clark, Victor. "Man of Discretion; Learning the Job
       in Northumberland." Times Educational Supplement
       2781:385, 9/6/68.
C41   Clements, Clyde C., Jr. "Unprofessional Mr. Crane."
       Pennsylvania School Journal 120:28-9, 9/71.
C42   Cohen, Ronald D. "Making a Curriculum; an Allegory."
       Improving College and University Teaching 19:341-4,
       Autumn 1971.
C43   Cohodes, Aaron. "Keep the Board Member and Fire
       the Board's Lawyer." Nation's Schools 88:12, 7/71.
C44   Cole, Barry. "Business of Poetry in Residence."
       Times Educational Supplement 2934:11, 8/13/71.
       Cromwell, Ronald E. SEE: Laughery, W. W.
C45   Cummins, Walter. "Tragedy of Bobby Ray Potts."
       AAUP Bulletin 60:29-32, 3/74.
C46   Dalton, Elizabeth L. "Now There's a Teacher!" To-
       day's Education 57:50, 12/68.
C47   D'Angelo, Lou. "Old Horizons in Education." Saturday
       Review 54:67, 12/4/71.
C48   Darnall, David D. "Ulcer; Satire." Physical Educator
       27:78, 5/70.
C49   Daugherty, Bob. "Burning Issue." Education Digest
       35:35, 2/70.
C50   Davidson, James F. "Present Discontents: Eleven
       Proposals toward Campus Rest." Journal of Higher
       Education 41:123-31, 12/70.
C51   Davis, Terry. "Snake; My Friend, Immanuel Snakebur-
       den." College English 35:825-9, 4/74.
C52   Demanche, Sister Edna. "Caging and Care of Young
       Octopi; a Bit of Whimsy." Science and Children 9:
       16/17, 5/72.
C53   DePue, Palmer. "Here We Go Round the Dullberry
       Bush." Educational Forum 33:485-9, 5/69.
C54   Derman, Samuel. "Wicked King and the Beautiful Prin-
       cess." Physics Teacher 9:387-8, 10/71.
C55   Diederich, Paul B. "27 Ways to Run Away from an
       Educational Problem." Today's Education 57:42-3,
       11/68.

C56 Dobbs, Stephen Mark. "Leave the Teaching to Us!"
     Phi Delta Kappan 53:back cover, 6/72.
C57 Doing, Larrie Anne. "All about My Mother the Board-
     man." American School Board Journal 159:40+,
     4/72.
C58 Domnick, Howard. "What This Generation Needs Is a
     Rousing Chorus of the Woodshed Blues." Today's
     Education 58:38-9, 4/69.
C59 Doolittle, H. "Pedagogic Palavers of Mrs. Dimit."
     College English 36:100-1, 9/74.
C60 Dovey, Irma. "Weathering the Storm (a Christmas In-
     cident at Hiawatha School)." Elementary English 46:
     1031-2, 12/69.
C61 DuBearn, Roger. "Scholarship." American Scholar
     37:307-10, Spring 1968.
C62 Dunlop, Richard S. "Typical Gaffes and Faux Pas
     Common among Beginning Counselor Trainees."
     Personnel and Guidance Journal 47:71+, 9/68.
C63 Dunn, Harold. "I Know What a Sextet Is, but I'd Rath-
     er Not Say." Today's Education 61:49, 11/72.
C64 _____. "Youngsterisms about Music." Today's Ed-
     ucation 57:61, 10/68.
     Dunne, Faith. SEE: Kelman, Peter.
C65 Ellis, H. F. "Young Men Remember." New Yorker
     44:40-1, 9/28/68.
C66 English, Fenwick W. "Freedom Halt; an Alternative
     School." Phi Delta Kappan 55:683-4, 6/74.
C67 Esquire. "Puke Ethics." Esquire 72:100-1, 9/69.
C68 Fensch, Edwin A. "Little Black Book." Clearing
     House 46:431-3, 3/72.
C69 Fisher, Eleanore. "What Is a Teacher?" Instructor
     79:23, 5/70.
C70 Fisher, Robert. "Project Slow Down: the Middle-
     Class Answer to Project Head Start." School and
     Society 98:356-7, 10/70.
C71 Flanagan, John A. "Tales of the American Classroom."
     Contemporary Education 45:149-54, Winter 1974.
C72 Flesch, Hugo. "Son of Why Johnny Can't Read and
     What You Can Do about It, by Hugo Flesch, Son of
     Rudolf Flesch, Author of the Father of Son of Why
     Johnny Can't Read and..." Wilson Library Bulletin
     45:270-1, 11/70.
C73 Foley, Teresa. "How the Whole Jar Got Spilled."
     Today's Education 63:61, 1/74.
C74 Forest, Robert. "Nostalgia Caper." Independent
     School Bulletin 34:49-54, 10/74.
C75 Forgan, Harry W. "Teachers Don't Want to Be

Labeled." Phi Delta Kappan 55:back cover, 9/73.

C76   Gardner, Theodosia. "Sex School Dropout." Saturday
      Review Education 1:5-6, 4/73.

C77   Giltinan, Betty. "I Wish I Hadn't Said That!" Today's
      Education 58:27, 4/69.

C78   Goldman, Joan. "Them Foreigners." Times Educa-
      tional Supplement 2883:4, 8/21/70.

C79   Gowin, Sarah. "Why? Why? Why?" Educational
      Forum 37:107, 11/72.

C80   Grandjouan, Claireve. "Dormouse Caper." AAUP
      Bulletin 60:27-8, 3/74.

C81   Graves, Wallace B. "Strategies for a Real Academic
      Revolution." Today's Education 59:26-7, 9/70.

C82   Greenberg, D. S. "Academic Protocol: from the
      Grant Swinger Manual." Science 170:47, 10/2/70.

C83   Griffin, Gary A. "Dehumanizing the School through
      Curriculum Planning or Who Needs Hemlock?" Na-
      tional Elementary Principal 49:24-7, 5/70.

C84   Haney, John B. "Green Light for Professor Wheeler."
      AAUP Bulletin 54:371-3, 9/68.

C85   Hansen, Lee H. "Model for Subverting Management by
      Objectives." Phi Delta Kappan 55:260-1, 12/73.

      Hardin, W. J. SEE: Warren, Mary Ann.

C86   Harmin, Merrill and Simon, S. B. "Relevance and the
      Kissing Curriculum." National Elementary Princi-
      pal 50:40-3, 9/70.

      Harrell, Roger L. SEE: Burns, Richard.

C87   Harris, Richard. "Alumnus." Look 33:87, 4/29/69.

C88   Haywood, C. R. "Stall-Oppenberger Syndrome; A
      Fantasy." Record 70:269-72, 1/69.

C89   Heindel, Richard H. "Letter of Congratulations to a
      New University President." School and Society 98:
      408-10, 11/70.

C90   Henderson, Ed. "Little Worbl Who Ran Away." Na-
      tional Elementary Principal 50:66-7, 4/71.

C91   Hightower, Toby E. "Adventures of a 50-Year-Old
      Graduate Student." Intellect 101:302-3, 2/73.

C92   _____. "Coward's Guide for Those Who Seek a Ca-
      reer in Education." Clearing House 46:399-401,
      3/72.

C93   Hollifield, John H. "Fully Computerized High School."
      Phi Delta Kappan 55:258-60, 12/73.

C94   _____. "Goodbye, Old Eastern High." Today's
      Education 61:22-3, 4/72.

C95   _____. "How to Get Straight A's." Today's Educa-
      tion 61:47, 9/72.

C96   Holman, Truman. "Prescriptive Prepunishment:

Panacea for Pupil Problems." <u>National Elementary Principal</u> 49:59, 5/70.

C97 Horn, Gunnar. "Hooked on Committees." <u>Today's Education</u> 62:25, 5/73.

C98 Horowitz, Murray M. "How to Articulate Authoritarian Ability Factors." <u>School and Society</u> 96:138-40, 3/2/68.

C99 Houts, Paul L. "Day the Shrimp Began to Whistle." <u>National Elementary Principal</u> 48:2-3, 1/69.

C100 Idstein, Peter. "Great Train Robbery." <u>Phi Delta Kappan</u> 53:back cover, 12/71.

C101 Instructor. "You Never Really Know What's Going to Happen Next; Seven Vignettes." <u>Instructor</u> 82:36-41, 6/73.

C102 Irsfeld, John H. "Handbook for Teaching Assistants." <u>College English</u> 38:108-11, 9/74.

C103 Isaacs, Ann Fahe. "Giftedness, Wisdom, and It Happened in a Supermarket." <u>Gifted Child Quarterly</u> 16:55+, Spring 1972.

C104 Israel, Lee. "Dick and Jane Revisited; Primer for Non-Reading Inner City Teenagers." <u>Saturday Review</u> 53:12+, 2/21/70.

C105 James, Hugh. "Can You Fix This?" <u>Grade Teacher</u> 89:54-5, 2/72.

C106 _____. "Letter from the Loan Company." <u>Grade Teacher</u> 89:74, 4/72.

C107 _____. "Open Letter to the New Kid." <u>Teacher</u> 90:58+, 9/72.

C108 Jenkins, Jeanne. "Spring Is When." <u>Grade Teacher</u> 87:88-9, 4/70.

C109 Kassan, Lawrence. "Serpent in the Garden; a Bibliographical Essay." <u>Phi Delta Kappan</u> 54:261-5, 12/72.

C110 Kelman, Peter and Dunne, Faith. "Rent-a-Martyr, Inc.; an Interview in the Future." <u>Phi Delta Kappan</u> 53:236-7, 12/71; <u>Media and Methods</u> 9:81+, 9/72.

C111 Kerensky, V. M. "Contributions of Edsel Murphy to the Understanding of Educational Systems." <u>Phi Delta Kappan</u> 56:42, 9/74.

C112 Kezard, Yelnats, pseud. "Wildwood College Rejects Civil Defense." <u>Adult Leadership</u> 17:167-8, 10/68.

C113 Kirman, Joseph M. "Simulator's Simulation Kit." <u>Social Education</u> 37:299, 4/73.

Kirschenbaum, Howard. SEE: Simon, Sidney.

C114 Kirwan, John D. "Non Campus Mentis." <u>National Review</u> 24:42, 1/21/72.

C115 Koeppen, Arlene. "Judgment Unaware." <u>Counselor</u>

Education and Supervision 13:320-2, 6/74.

C116 Kohler, Carl. "Great Electron-Pedantic Project."
Popular Electronics 32:48-52, 2/70.

C117 Krawitz, Michael. "Head of the Class." Saturday Review 55:8, 1/15/72.

C118 Kwinn, David. "Educorp University in Tomorrowland."
Intellect 102:235-6, 1/74.

C119 Lacey, Richard L. "Chameleons." Today's Education 57:33, 9/68.

C120 Lamb, David. "Up the School; a Fashionable Game for Dice and Counter." Times Educational Supplement 2900:10+, 12/18/70.

C121 Laughery, W. W. and Cromwell, Ronald E. "Reflections of a Student Teacher." Journal of Teacher Education 21:34-43, Spring 1970.

C122 Lawrence, Bill. "American History Blown Off Course by Eighth Graders"; excerpts from Then Some Other Stuff Happened. Today's Education 58:51, 9/69.

C123 Lewis, Florence C. "Some of My Best Friends Are Counselors." Phi Delta Kappan 53:372-3, 2/72.

C124 Longe, Robert C. "Notes." Today's Education 60:40, 3/71.

C125 Longo, Paul. "Faculty at War." Phi Delta Kappan 55:back cover+, 5/74.

C126 Luttrell, Sally Alexander. "Proposal for a New Lexicon." College English 35:52, 10/73.

C127 MacBeth, Edwin. "I Was Only a Pawn on the Board of Education." Nation's Schools 93:10+, 3/74.

C128 MacKarell, Peter. "Introduction to the P. E. Staff."
Times Educational Supplement 2765:1678, 5/17/68.

C129 Makins, Virginia. "Child's Eye View of Teacher."
Times Educational Supplement 2835:21-2+, 9/19;
2836:18+, 9/26/69.

C130 Malcolm, Dave. "This I Beheld, or Dreamed It in a Dream, or Saw It through the Porthole of My Yellow Submarine." Counselor Education and Supervision 13:320, 6/74.

C131 Mallinson, George G. "Oh Where Is My Horse's Patoote?" School Science and Mathematics 73:705-6, 12/73.

C132 Marchie, Howard E. "Glossary of Administrative Birds." Clearing House 46:226, 12/71.

C133 Matzkin, Carol. "On Campus, Peacenik in the Center Ring." Mademoiselle 67:56+, 5/68.

C134 McClanahan, Sam F. "Professorial Upmanship." Contemporary Education 42:44, 10/70; 43:48-9, 10/71.

C135 McClure, Larry. "Birds to Look Out For; Ornithological Guide to School Reorganization." Phi Delta Kappan 51:back cover, 12/69.

C136 McCullough, Constance M. "Mess of Pottage." Reading Teacher 26:550-2, 3/73.

C137 McGuire, Vincent. "Florida Fable." English Journal 58:122-3, 1/69.

C138 McKinnis, Paul Willis. "Administrative Bulletin 2115-2A6-7935-17XP 1204536." Today's Education 59:41, 2/70.

C139 McQueen, Robert. "Look Over the Shoulder of a Scholarship Committee Chairman." Today's Education 59:446, 1/70.

C140 Middlebrook, Jonathan. "Finders Keepers." College English 32:605-9, 2/71.

C141 Miller, D. D. "On Earthquakes and Drowning Babies." School and Community 58:31, 5/72.

C142 _____. "Taking a Load of Goats to Fort Worth; or, How to Define the Problem." Phi Delta Kappan 55: 177, 11/73.

C143 Miller, William C. "Another Day." Educational Leadership 30:63-4, 10/72.

C144 Montgomery, James R. et al. "Typical U. Meets the Press." College and University Journal 11:30-1, 5/72.

C145 Moore, Billie. "Dizzyland of Show and Tell." Today's Education 59:57, 11/70.

C146 Moore, Richard W. "How Many Angels Can Dance on the Head of a Pin? Journal of General Education 26:159-60, Summer 1974.

C147 Motzkus, John F. "Welcome Back." Today's Education 62:81-2, 9/73.

C148 National Review. "Green Power: Irish Students at Queens College." National Review 21:216, 3/11/69.

C149 O'Donnell, R. W. "Swimmer-Training Institutions." Today's Education 61:54-5, 1/72.

C150 Ohliger, John. "Adult Education: 1984." Adult Leadership 19:223-4, 1/71.

C151 Ozman, Howard. "King Arthur and the Knights of the Accountable." Education 92:50, 11/71.

C152 Parks, Tom. "Our Next Speaker Needs No Introduction." English Journal 63:13, 4/74.

C153 Pearl, Arthur. "Hansel and Gretel; Life at an Alternative School." Saturday Review 55:51-2, 12/9/72.

C154 Pierce, Eleanor Beers. "My Riot: at the University of Wisconsin, 1937." Saturday Review 51:4+, 5/18/68.

C155 Pinck, Dan. "Madrid Plan." Saturday Review Education 1:68-9, 5/73.

C156 Primack, Robert. "If Horace Mann Belonged to the
        SDS." Phi Delta Kappan 51:99-100, 10/69.

C157 Quinn, Mildred. "September Song." Business Educa-
        tion World 49:13-14, 9/68.

C158 Rall, Eilene M. "My Regards to Ustinov." English
        Journal 58:548-60, 4/69.

C159 Read, Lawrence F. "Lobby Triumphs: Knitting Con-
        quers All; Satire." Clearing House 43:35-9, 9/68.

C160 Reese, Willard F. "We Don't Want No Boat Rockers."
        Phi Delta Kappan 50:232-5, 12/68.

C161 Richstone, May. "Where Is This Thing Called Poise?"
        Grade Teacher 89:46-7+, May-June 1972.

C162 Riemer, George. "Dehumanization and Subsequent
        Radicalization of Young Dylan Lazerbeeme, Defacer,
        Graffitist, Aerosol Sloganist and Obscenario Writer,
        Free-Lance and Underground; a Closet Drama in
        Three Grim Acts and Six Grisly Grades." National
        Elementary Principal 49:13-23, 5/70.

C163 Robinson, Thomas E. "One a Penny, Two a Penny."
        Today's Education 58:61, 1/69.

C164 Romano, Ralph P. "Lots of People Think They See
        Flying Saucers." Phi Delta Kappan 51:444-5, 4/70.

C165 Rosenau, Fred. "Fog Lifts; Satire." Phi Delta Kappan
        54:back cover, 3/73.

C166 Rosten, Leo. "Leo Rosten's Handy-Dandy Plan to Save
        Our Colleges." Look 34:76+, 12/15/70.

C167 Ruffing, Robert R. "Ruffing Rule (Why Things Can Nev
        er Be the Same Again)." Phi Delta Kappan 55:439,
        2/74.

C168 Sadker, Myra. "Education of El Toot." National Ele-
        mentary Principal 49:28-30, 5/70.

C169 Sanna, Joanne. "What Is a First Grader?" Instructor
        81:136, 2/72.

C170 Sarver, Phillip M. "Proposal to Change College Course
        Offerings." Contemporary Education 45:68, Fall
        1973.

C171 Saxe, Richard W. "Understanding the Graffiti." Phi
        Delta Kappan 51:344, 2/70.

C172 Schoenstein, Ralph. "Day that Revolution Became One
        of the Three R's." Today's Health 49:48-9, 11/71.

C173 Simmons, Daniel J. "Beware! the Three R's Cometh."
        Phi Delta Kappan 54:492-5, 3/73.

    Simon, S. B. SEE: Harmin, Merrill.

C174 Simon, Sidney and Kirschenbaum, Howard. "Ultimate
        Grading Game." Phi Delta Kappan 53:443, 3/72.

C175 Simpson, Jerry H., Jr. "Place Where I Belong At."

Today's Education 59:71, 9/70.
C176 Smith, Lois Ann. "Bestiary for Educators." Contemporary Education 45:69-71, Fall 1973.
C177 Spears, Harold. "Fallow Season." Education Digest 38:36-7, 11/72.
C178 Spencer, William A. "Likely Story." College and University Journal 12:43-4+, 5/73.
C179 Squires, Raymond. "Turning Out Non-Readers; with Study-Discussion Program." PTA Magazine 64:6-8, 9/69.
C180 Stanton, Will. "Bring Back the Stork!" Good Housekeeping 177:59-60+, 8/73.
C181 _____. "Rumpelstiltskin, He Said His Name Was." Reader's Digest 95:51-3, 8/69.
C182 Stapleton, Peg. "Once Upon a Cold Wintry Day." Teacher 90:12, 3/73.
C183 Stevens, John M. "Competency-Based Education and Its Enemies." Phi Delta Kappan 55:back cover+, 1/74.
C184 Stigler, George. "Truth in Teaching; Liability for Material Taught." National Review 25:737-8, 7/6/73.
C185 Stowell, Shirley. "Trouble with Teachers as Seen through the Eyes of the School Secretary." Ohio Schools 47:18-19, 2/14/69.
C186 Styza, C. J. "Specialist." Phi Delta Kappan 49:inside cover, 6/68.
C187 Suggs, Keith. "Sweeney Goes to School." Phi Delta Kappan 56:54-7, 9/74.
Taylor, Halsey. SEE: Allen, Don
C188 Tebbe, Nancy. "Escape from Teaching to Motherhood." Phi Delta Kappan 55:480-1, 3/74.
C189 Teitel, Nathan. "Learning at Night." Saturday Review Education 1:11-12, 5/73.
C190 Thyme, Mae. "Bad Day at Wild Rose." Today's Health 48:58-9+, 11/70.
C191 Time. "Where Are You, Helga Sue?" Time 102:46, 7/16/73.
C192 Times Educational Supplement. "Chalk Stage." Times Educational Supplement 2760:1211, 4/12/68.
C193 _____. "Those Were the Days, My Friend." Times Educational Supplement 2800:135, 1/17/69.
C194 Tobias, Jeraihmiel. "Teacher and the Birds." Contemporary Education 45:76-7, Fall 1973.
C195 Today's Education. "Light Touch." Today's Education 57:33, 9/68; 61, 10/68; 42-3, 11/68; 50, 12/68.
C196 _____. "Negotiation Game." Today's Education 59:54-5, 4/70.

C197 Toler, Wilma M. "Please Leave Your Papers on the
      Stove!" Business Education World 49:21, 3/69.
C198 Trow, William Clark. "Great Revolt in Higher Educa-
      tion." School and Society 96:372-3, 10/26/68.
C199 Turney, David. "Rights of Spring." Contemporary
      Education 43:355, 5/72.
C200 Unick, Sal Peter, pseud. "Reducing Sexual Desire;
      Satire." Personnel and Guidance Journal 48:851-2,
      6/70.
C201 Van Til, William. "Horace Mann's Only Appearance
      on TV." Phi Delta Kappan 54:411, 2/73.
C202 _____. "Wonderland Is a Strange Place." Phi
      Delta Kappan 50:inside back cover, 5/69.
C203 Wachowiak, Dale G. "Go West, Man; a Dream Frag-
      ment." Personnel and Guidance Journal 52:102-4,
      10/73.
C204 Wack, R. Donald. "It's Time to Tear Down the Old
      Hotel." Clearing House 44:504-5, 4/70.
C205 Warren, Mary Ann and Hardin, W. J. "First-of-the-
      Year Horoscope for Teachers." Teacher 91:49,
      9/73.
C206 Weldy, Gilbert R. "Fellow Principals, Unite!" Clear-
      ing House 44:214-19, 12/69.
C207 Williams, Frank B., Jr. "Psalter for a Faculty Meet-
      ing." Educational Record 49:296-7, Fall 1968.
C208 Williams, Gary Jay. "Memo from Osiris." National
      Review 25:1061, 9/28/73.
C209 Wilson, Charles H. "Day Mrs. Levinson Spindled the
      Kindergarteners' IBM Cards." Phi Delta Kappan
      50:432-3, 3/69.
C210 Woods, June. "Efficiency at All Costs!" Today's Edu-
      cation 59:19, 2/70.
C211 Woolf, Leonard. "Modern Fable for Educators."
      Educational Forum 36:545, 5/72.
C212 Workman, Brooke. "Mission Impossible." Today's
      Education 61:53, 12/72.
C213 Wright, Betty. "Biology at Its Best." Good House-
      keeping 169:173, 7/69.
C214 Yeingst, Robert. "Wizard of AV." Audiovisual In-
      struction 18:92-3, 3/73.
C215 Zimmerman, James. "Test." Illinois Education 59:
      107+, 2/71.
C216 Zinsser, William Knowlton. "Commencement Address."
      Life 64:27, 5/24/68.

HEALTH, SAFETY, MEDICAL SCIENCES,
AND PSYCHOLOGY

D1   Ace, Goodman. "Defilling the Prescription; Plans for New Labeling of Prescription Drugs." Saturday Review 54:4, 5/8/71.

D2   _____. "Hummmming." Saturday Review 54:6, 8/14/71.

D3   _____. "Needling the Doctor." Saturday Review 52: 7, 3/8/69.

D4   _____. "Patient." Saturday Review 54:8, 9/25/71.

D5   _____. "Young Names Makes News." Saturday Review 53:12, 10/10/70.

D6   Adler, Bill. "Dear Baby Doctor"; excerpts from Mothers Write Funny Letters to Baby Doctors. Today's Health 48:24-6, 9/70; 75-6, 10/70.

D7   Allen, Woody. "Metterling Lists." New Yorker 45: 34-5, 5/10/69.

D8   _____. "Notes from the Overfed." New Yorker 44: 38-9, 3/16/68.

D9   American Journal of Clinical Nutrition. "Serum Cholesterol--the Etiology of Disease." American Journal of Clinical Nutrition 23:413-9, 4/70.

Amite, pseud. SEE: Foley, Gardner P. H.

D10   Andrews, D. "Outpatient Department." Nursing Mirror and Midwives Journal 130:42, 1/30/70.

D11   Arlen, Michael J. "Standing in the Wind." McCall's 99:54+, 10/71.

D12   Armour, Richard. "Confessions of a Cold-Cure Collector." Reader's Digest 99:55-6, 10/71.

D13   _____. "Discovery of an Unpublished Manuscript." Journal of the American Medical Association 204:59-60, 4/1/68 (book section).

D14   _____. "Distant Shaves: Memories of Blades Past." Saturday Review 55:4, 5/27/72.

D15   _____. "Is Dr. Doctor In?" Reader's Digest 99: 114-5, 7/71.

D16   _____. "Short Note on Long Hair." Saturday Re-
       view 54:4, 6/19/71.

D17   Ashworth, Henry. "Friends and Neighbors." Man-
       chester Medical Gazette 51:76-7, 4/72.

D18   Baker, Russell. "Good Things that Undone Poor Gum."
       Life 67:16B, 8/15/69.

D19   _____. "Medicar." New York Times Magazine p.
       6, 7/7/74.

D20   _____. "Redress." New York Times Magazine p.
       6, 12/8/74.

D21   Barnes, Sheila. "Tulley Knows Best!" Nursing Mir-
       ror and Midwives Journal 135:14, 7/21/72.

D22   Bartholomew, M. K. "Dig That Crazy Lamp." Nurs-
       ing Mirror and Midwives Journal 136:21, 3/30/73.

D23   Beaumont, Mary. "Memory of Cass." Nursing Mirror
       and Midwives Journal 136:24, 1/19/73.

D24   Beddoes, Ruth. "Dry Rot." Nursing Times 66:1086,
       8/20/70.

D25   Bennett, Margaret, pseud. "Through the Tube Darkly:
       Telecontraception." Harper's 245:115-6+, 11/72.

D26   Bentley, C. "The Rational Physician; Richard Whit-
       lock's Medical Satires." Journal of the History of
       Medicine and Allied Sciences 29:180-95, 4/74.

D27   Berde, B. "Singularities: The Audacious and the
       Scrupulous Pharmacologist or Why Congresses Are
       Unprecedented Successes or Downright Catastrophes."
       Agents and Actions 2:156-7, 11/71.

D28   Berger, Dean M. Letter: "The Extraordinary Case
       of the Blue Hands." Journal of the American Medi-
       cal Association 229:522-3, 7/29/74.

D29   Bernstein, Leonard S. "Worry Level." House Beauti-
       ful 114:76+, 11/72.

D30   Bishop, Dorothy. "How to Be ... a New/Old Nurse."
       Nursing Mirror and Midwives Journal 135:14-5,
       9/15/72.

D31   Blackmore, D. K. et al. "Some Observations on the
       Diseases of Brunus Edwardii (Species Nova)." Vet-
       erinary Record 90:382-5, 4/1/72; discussion, 90:
       428, 462-4, 492, 521, 641-2, 692, 4/8-29, 5/27,
       6/10/72.

D32   Bluestone, N. "Clarence Barton, R.N." Supervisor
       Nurse 4:21+, 10/73.

D33   Bocca, Geoffrey. "Exciting Adventures in Bad Eating."
       Esquire 71:80+, 5/69.

D34   Bombeck, Erma. "Forgetting to Remember." Good
       Housekeeping 172:38+, 5/71.

D35   _____. "Give In to a Cold? Not Me!" Good

Housekeeping 172:48+, 3/71.

D36 _____. "Great Hair Switch." Good Housekeeping
170:16+, 1/70.

D37 _____. "Never Say Drive!" Good Housekeeping
170: 26+, 5/70.

D38 Bornemeier, Walter C. "Grandpa's Grandpa." West
Virginia Medical Journal 67:183-4, 7/71.

D39 Brickman, Marshall. "Kentish Sleep Journal." New
Yorker 50:36-7, 9/16/74.

D40 Brien, Alan. "Dead Is a Four-Letter Word." Holiday
43:8+, 4/68.

D41 Brown, Bob. "Effect of the Bureaucracy on Automobiles." Car and Driver 19:6, 5/74.

D42 Bruce, Jeannette. "Cook It Up and Dish It Out; Organic Food." Sports Illustrated 38:42-4+, 2/19/73.

D43 Buchwald, Art. "Art Buchwald Crash-Diet Plan."
Reader's Digest 102:95-6, 6/73.

D44 _____. "Scholastis Adolescum: A Disease Every
Kid Has the Cure For"; excerpts from Sons of the
Great Society. Today's Health 49:44-5, 9/71.

D45 Carpenter, Elizabeth. "Love Means Never Having to
Say You're Starving; Reducing Ranches." McCall's
99:63+, 7/72.

D46 Carr, Mary. "Those Were the Days." Nursing Times
68:1138, 9/7/72.

D47 Changing Times, "Pooped Generation." Changing
Times 23:7-11, 12/69.

D48 Chapman, Graham. "Some Medical Recollections--and
Others." Manchester Medical Gazette 52:10, 10/72.

D49 Chichester, Francis. "Keeping Fit with Sir Francis
Chichester." Esquire 71:98-101+, 6/69.

D50 Ciardi, John. "On Being Brave." Saturday Review
World 1:37, 7/13/74.

D51 Cobb, Irvin Shrewsbury. "Speaking of Operations."
Saturday Evening Post 245:36-41+, 5/73.

D52 Cohen, Anthea. "A Minor Operation Takes No Time
at All." Nursing Mirror and Midwives Journal 128:
44+, 3/7/69.

D53 _____. "Nurses Are Not Neurotic." Canadian
Nurse 65:45, 6/69; Nursing Mirror and Midwives
Journal 128:32, 2/7/69.

D54 Coleman, Vernon. "The Accident." Nursing Times
68:689, 6/1/72.

D55 _____. "Bleep Bleep!" Nursing Times 68:587,
5/11/72.

D56 _____. "Hunting Season." Nursing Times 68:
1105, 8/31/72.

D57 _____. "Mrs. Norris." Nursing Times 69:387, 3/22/73.

D58 _____. "My Girl's a Nurse..." Nursing Mirror and Midwives Journal 134:17, 6/2/72; 43, 6/9/72; 22, 6/16/72; 29, 6/23/72; 39, 6/30/72; 135:45, 7/7/72; 38, 7/14/72; 37, 7/21/72; 38, 7/28/72; 30, 8/4/72.

D59 _____. "The NHS Alphabet." Nursing Times 68: 1622-5, 12/21/72.

D60 _____. "The New Ward." Nursing Times 68:657, 5/25/72.

D61 _____. "Night-Cell." Nursing Times 68:788, 6/22/72.

D62 Crawshaw, Ralph. "What to Do with the Bean from a Patient's Ear." Archives of Internal Medicine 131: 278-9, 2/73.

D63 Cronk, Hilary M. "Ask Auntie Hilary..." Nursing Times 69:293, 3/1/73.

D64 _____. "The Body-Snatchers." Nursing Times 68: 1199-1200, 9/21/72.

D65 _____. "Dame School." Nursing Times 66:1113+, 8/27/70.

D66 _____. "Off the Boil." Nursing Times 65:864+, 7/3/69.

D67 Davis, Paul J. and Gregerman, Robert I. "Parse Analysis: A New Method for the Evaluation of Investigators' Bibliographies." New England Journal of Medicine 281:989-90, 10/30/69.

D68 Davis, Philip J. "Left Lib, Right Lib." National Review 25:32+, 1/5/73.

D69 Dawson, Renata. "The Deep End." Nursing Times 66:1118, 8/27/70.

D70 Deery, Arthur. "At the Receiving End." Medical Journal of Australia 2:102-5, 7/8/72.

D71 Dentibus, E. X. and Ensis, R. A. D. C. "Accountomania Computococcus; the Results of Infection with the Newly Discovered." Manchester Medical Gazette 51:120-1, 7/72.

Derby, George H. SEE: Foley, Gardner P. H.

D72 Doering, E. J. III; Fitts, C. T.; and Rambo, W. M. "Alligator Bite." Journal of the American Medical Association 218:255-6, 10/11/71.

D73 Drew, M. E. "Things Fall Apart." Nursing Mirror and Midwives Journal 134:14, 6/2/72.

D74 Dunes, George. "Healthspeak for All Seasons." Journal of the American Medical Association 229:436, 7/22/74.

D75 Eggers, William T. "Staff Humor in Our Homes."
 Professional Nursing Home 10:36+, 6/68.
D76 Einstein, Stanley. "The Drug Game." International
 Journal of Addictions 7:395-8, Summer 1972.
D77 Eisenman, Russell. "How to Be a Rigid, Dogmatic
 Therapist." Psychological Reports 22:904, 6/68
 Part I.
D78 Ellis, H. F. "Visual Welfare State." New Yorker
 45:103-4+, 4/19/69.
D79 Elwarf, Y. "Teratogenicity of Muscas Domesticas
 Swaticas (MDS)." Food and Cosmetics Toxicology
 8:717-8, 12/70.
 Ensis, R. A. D. C. SEE: Dentibus, E. X.
D80 Ephron, Nora. "Few Words about Breasts." Esquire
 77:95-7+, 5/72; reprint, 80:278-80+, 10/73.
D81 Esquire. "Happy Days for You! August 1969." Es-
 quire 72:68-9, 8/69.
D82 Finlay, Mike. "Bleep... Bleep... Bleep--Life in Resi-
 dence." Manchester Medical Gazette 53:9-10, 12/73.
D83 _____. "What Is a Medical Student?" Manchester
 Medical Gazette 51:54-7, 1/72.
D84 Fischer, John. "Vital Signs." Harper's 249:28-30,
 8/74.
D85 Fisher-Pap, Lucia. Editorial: "Medical Abbrevia-
 tions--the Language of Obscurity." Annals of Al-
 lergy 32:257-8, 5/74.
 Fitts, C. T. SEE: Doering, E. J.
D86 Foley, Gardner P. H. "Dentistry and the Nineteenth
 Century American Humorists. 2. 'Dental Surgery,'
 by Amite." New York Journal of Dentistry 38:361-
 2, 10/68.
D87 _____. "Dentistry and the Nineteenth Century American Humorists. 4. 'Tushmaker's Toothpuller,' by
 George H. Derby." New York Journal of Dentistry
 38:439-40, 12/68.
D88 _____. "Dentistry and the Nineteenth Century American Humorists. 5. 'Bill Whiffletree's Dental Experience,' by Jonathan F. Kelley." New York Journal of Dentistry 39:12-4, 1/69.
D89 _____. "Dentistry and the Nineteenth Century American Humorists. 3. 'The Mississippi Patent Plan
 for Pulling Teeth,' by Henry Clay Lewis." New
 York Journal of Dentistry 38:404-6, 11/68.
D90 _____. "Dentistry and the Nineteenth Century American Humorists." 1. 'Incident at Natchez,' by Sol
 Smith." New York Journal of Dentistry 38:322-4,
 8-9/68.

D91   Foraker, Alvan G. "The Last Uterus." Obstetrics
      and Gynecology 43:153-5, 1/74.
D92   _____. "The Temptation of Dr. Faust--1971."
      Perspectives in Biology and Medicine 14:473-6,
      Spring 1971.
D93   Ford, Corey. "Ford's Physical Unfitness Program."
      Reader's Digest 94:80-2, 5/69.
D94   _____. "Get Lost!" Field & Stream 73:5+, 11/68.
D95   G. F. --Vox Populi, pseud. "A Pre-Medical Reaction."
      Manchester Medical Gazette 51:42-3, 1/72.
D96   Gallagher, John J. and Gallagher, Anna Helen. "A
      Phantasy (with References)." American Journal of
      Nursing 70:538+, 3/70.
D97   Gillespie, Bete. "Fathers Only Journals; Public Dia-
      ries in Hospital Obstetrical Wards." Today's Health
      47:17-18, 12/69.
D98   Golomb, Solomon W. "Patient Etiquette." Saturday
      Review Science 1:10-11, 5/73.
D99   Greengold, Myron C. "Letter from Copenhagen."
      Journal of the American Medical Association 204:
      57-8, 4/1/68.
D100 Grigg, Kenneth N. "The Book of Genesis and Mental
      Health." Medical Journal of Australia 2:1339, 12/
      25/71.
D101 Hackett, Earle. "Christmas Disease." Medical Jour-
      nal of Australia 2:1261-3, 12/26/70.
D102 Hall, R. Norton. "Massa Hoax." College of Physi-
      cians, Philadelphia. Transactions and Studies. 37:
      286-90, 4/70.
D103 Harper's Bazaar. "How to Make a Great Getaway."
      Harper's Bazaar 102:214-5, 5/69.
D104 Hash, John H. "Lysosomes and Lysozymes." Molecu-
      lar and Cellular Biochemistry 2:103, 11/15/73.
D105 Heilman, Robert B. "Holiday Highway Deaths Fall Be-
      low Record." American Scholar 43:55-65, Winter
      1973.
D106 Hulka, J. F. "Multichannel Automatic Natality Sensor
      with Instantaneous Computer-Integrator and Audio-
      visual Recorder; a New Instrument." Obstetrics and
      Gynecology 37:155-7, 1/71.
D107 Hulme, Judd. "The Incredible Footbath Mystery."
      Nursing Mirror and Midwives Journal 137:28-9, 8/
      24/73.
D108 Johns, M. "The First Days of Creation of a Medical
      Paper." New Zealand Medical Journal 74:347, 11/71.
D109 Jones, Alfred. "The Driving Lesson." Nursing Mirror
      and Midwives Journal 131:50, 10/9/70.

D110 Jones, Mary. "On Call." Nursing Times 68:1626-7,
    12/21/72.
D111 Keillor, Garrison. "Bangor Man." New Yorker 48:
    39, 10/14/70.
    Kelley, Jonathan F. SEE: Foley, Gardner P. H.
D112 Keniston, Kenneth. "How Community Mental Health
    Stamped Out the Riots (1968-78)." Trans-Action 5:
    20-9, 7/68.
D113 Kilby-Kelberg, Sally. "Aunt Libby and Her Cure-Alls.
    American Journal of Nursing 73:1056-7, 6/73.
D114 Kinzer, David M. "The Unmerciful Grilling of Gurtz,
    or the Way It's Going to Be." Modern Hospital
    119:81-91, 7/72.
D115 Klassen, William. "Beard." Christian Century 85:
    993, 8/7/68.
D116 Kohler, Carl. "Kool-Keeping Kwiz." Popular Elec-
    tronics 32:63-4, 6/70.
D117 Laerum, Ole Didrik and Skullerud, Kari. "Morbidity
    in Assistants." Canadian Medical Association Jour-
    nal 110:632-3, 3/16/74.
D118 Lamp. "Non-Unionist's Psalm." Lamp 28:19, 10/71.
D119 Lane, T. "Rebel's Solution." Nursing Mirror and
    Midwives Journal 135:48, 10/6/72.
D120 Lawrence, Barbara. "Patient." New Yorker 50:162-
    8, 11/4/74.
D121 Levenson, Sam. "My Farewell to Girth Control."
    Ladies' Home Journal 88:116+, 5/71.
D122 _____. "Oh, Doctor!" Ladies' Home Journal 87:
    64+, 10/70.
    Lewis, Henry Clay. SEE: Foley, Gardner P. H.
D123 Luccock, Hatford Edward. "Transplanted Heads."
    Christian Century 85:407, 3/27/68.
D124 Ludvigsen, Karl E. "Racers on the Road." Motor
    Trend 21:32-5, 3/69.
D125 Mademoiselle. "Zoo Game: Quiz that Tells You What
    Kind of a Beast You Are." Mademoiselle 75:143-
    5+, 6/72.
D126 Magee, Mary. "Mary Magee to Sister D." American
    Journal of Nursing 69:74+, 1/69.
D127 Main, A. W. "Pussy and the Pill." Medical Journal
    of Australia 2:1462-3, 12/23/72.
D128 Martin, M. W. "Dubious Definitions." Nursing '73,
    3:33, 11/73.
D129 _____. "Dubious Definitions." Nursing '74, 4:46,
    1/74.
D130 Maslin, Mary. "Pen Portraits of People. 'The Vic-
    ar's Wife'." Nursing Mirror and Midwives Journal

136:28, 2/23/73.

D131 _____. "Pen Portraits of People. 'The VIP'."
Nursing Mirror and Midwives Journal 136:25, 3/2/73

D132 McGuckin, P. "The Other Side of the Fence." Radiography 38:58, 3/72.

D133 McGuire, Sarah. "An Apple (or Something) a Day."
Nursing Times 69:944, 7/19/73.

D134 McLean, John. "The Night of the Red Devil." Nursing Mirror and Midwives Journal 134:22, 5/26/72.

D135 McManus, Patrick F. "Rescue." Field & Stream 77: 80+, 2/73.

D136 Middleton, Thomas H. "What's the Square Root of Supercolossal?" Saturday Review World 1:74, 10/23/73.

D137 Morgan, Kenneth R. "Gone But Not Forgotten." Nursing '74, 4:14-15, 4/74.

D138 Mosier, D. E. "The Tale of Dr. Nathaniel Crooke or On the Existence of Autoimmune States." Perspectives in Biology and Medicine 13:108-14, Autumn 1969.

D139 Munson, Don. "Homo Sapiens Amphibialus; or, Man and His Tubs." House Beautiful 110:79+, 3/68.

D140 Murphy, Richard W. "On Breathing and Other Ills."
Harper's 242:22+, 5/71.

D141 National Review. "Automotive Perfecta." National Review 25:1041, 9/28/73.

D142 Nelson, Robert S. "Endoscopic Vignettes." Gastrointestinal Endoscopy 17:185, 5/71.

D143 Nursing Times. "Carry On from Here, Nurse." Nursing Times 68:1356, 10/26/72.

D144 Ober, William B. "A Modest Proposal for Preventing Choriocarcinoma among Innocent Mothers." Obstetrics and Gynecology 31:866-9, 6/68.

D145 O'Donnell, Richard W. "Sad, Sad Tale." National Review 23:369, 4/6/71.

D146 Olendzki, M. "Into Orbit." Journal of Nursing Administration 1:41-3, 11-12/71.

D147 _____. "The White Cat's Tale." Journal of Nursing Administration 2:25-8, 3-4/72.

D148 O'Neill, Susan Kramer. "Childbirth by the Book."
RN Magazine 36:42-4, 7/73.

Osler, William. SEE: Tigertt, W. D.

D149 Patel, M. D. "To Write a Paper." Journal of the Indian Medical Association 60:68-70, 1/16/73.

D150 Pearse, Warren H. "Faculty Assessment and Review."
Obstetrics and Gynecology 42:146-8, 7/73.

D151 Phinney, Jan C. "Art of Successfully Getting Lost."

Field & Stream 73:60-1+, 5/68.

D152 Piper, Doris A. "Weightless Ward." American Journal of Nursing 68:2360+, 11/68.

D153 Point of View. "How Do You... When and Where Are the Preoperative Shave Preps of Patients Done in Your Hospital?" Point of View 10:16, n.2, 1973.

D154 Poltroon, Milford. "How I Stopped Smoking and Had Fun Doing It." Atlantic Monthly 221:112-15, 3/68.

D155 Powles, William E. "A Martian Psychiatrist Views with Alarm the Current State of the Term "Schizophrenia'." Diseases of the Nervous System 29:Supplement 5-10, 5/68.

D156 Quinn, Robert E. "Improving Your Doctor." Today's Health 46:38-9, 9/68.

D157 Radiography. "Mrs. Beeton's Basic Knee Joint." Radiography 37:116-7, 5/71.

Rambo, W. M. SEE: Doering, E. J.

D158 Reich, Nathaniel E. "The Doctor as an Organization Man." Perspectives in Biology and Medicine 16: 308-11, Winter 1973.

D159 Rivers, Joan. "I'm Glad I'm a Middle-Aged Sex Object." McCall's 99:78+, 10/71.

D160 Rose, Ian. "Lectureshipmanship." Canadian Medical Association Journal 101:114-6, 10/4/69.

D161 Rowe, P. N. "Sometimes Pertinent, Sometimes Impertinent, but Nevertheless an Adventure." Lancet 1:875-6, 4/21/73.

D162 Russotto, Joseph S. "Dieting: Mind Over Platter." Harvest Years 8:22-3, 7/68.

D163 Saddler, Harry. "Medical Tidbits." AORN Journal 17:75-6, 3/73.

D164 Sagoff, Maurice. "At Sea with the Owl and the Pussycat." Mademoiselle 66:199+, 2/68.

D165 Samson, Edward. "Just a Thought." British Dental Journal 132:243-4, 3/21/72.

D166 Saroyan, William. "Apple Pie and Crazy People." Nation 213:629-30, 12/13/71.

D167 Sather, Mary A. "Down the Halls with Wrench and Screwdriver." American Journal of Nursing 73: 1186-7, 7/73.

D168 School Safety. "Would You Believe?" School Safety 4:10-11, 3/69.

D169 Scott, P. J. "By Nurse and Machine." New Zealand Nursing Journal 66:8-12, 7/73.

D170 Shepherd, Jean. Column. Car and Driver 20:10 +, 8/74.

D171 Sheppard, Eugenia. "How Well You Look!" Harper's

Bazaar 102:168-9, 8/69.
D172 _____. "On Being a Blonde." Harper's Bazaar
102:204-5, 9/69.
D173 Skinner, Cornelia Otis. "My, O Myopia!" Reader's
Digest 100:37-8+, 5/72.
D174 Smiley, C. W. "How to Fail as a Therapist." South
African Medical Journal 48:37-8, 1/12/74.
D175 Smith, Shawn Q. M. "Sic Transit Gloria Swanson
(Hippocrates Has a Lot to Answer For)." Man-
chester Medical Gazette 51:47-8, 1/72.
Smith, Sol. SEE: Foley, Gardner P. H.
D176 Stanley, N. F.; Stanley, E. R.; Stanley, Fiona; and
Stanley, Pamela. "The Brolga Bites Back." Medi-
cal Journal of Australia 2:1461-2, 12/23/72.
D177 Stanton, Will. "Home Is Where the Harm Is."
Reader's Digest 103:169-72, 10/73.
D178 _____. "Perils of a Procrastinator." Reader's Di-
gest 104:102-5, 1/74.
D179 _____. "Put Your Best Foot Backward." Reader's
Digest 103:91-3, 12/73.
D180 Stevens, S. W. "Say 'Ah-gwah-ching.'" Nursing Care
6:21, 3/73.
D181 Stewart, B. "Classics from the Classroom." Nurs-
ing Care 6:19-20, 10/73.
D182 Sturgeon, Theodore. "I Love Maple Walnut." Harper's
248:103, 5/74.
D183 Swinnerton, A. R. "Let's Get Organized." Retirement
Living 13:40-1, 11/73.
D184 Thomas, Michael. "Big P." Look 33:14+, 4/15/69.
D185 Tigertt, W. D. "Annotated Answers to the 1902 Exam-
ination on Osler's Principles and Practice of Medi-
cine." Annals of Internal Medicine 79:460-72, 9/73.
D186 Toman, Sue W. "Following Procedures." American
Journal of Nursing 73:280-1, 2/73.
D187 Tomkins, Calvin. "Mu: Breath Control Exercises in
Your Automobile while You Are Stuck in Traffic."
New Yorker 46:53, 12/5/70.
D188 Trahey, Jane. "These Drinks Are on Me!" Harper's
Bazaar 103:190-200, 12/69.
D189 Vaisrub, Samuel. Editorial: "Laughing All the Way to
the Bank." Journal of the American Medical Asso-
ciation 229:193, 7/8/74.
D190 _____. "The Revolutionary Scalpel." Diseases of
the Chest 55:444-5, 6/69.
D191 Van Dine, Alan. "Minutes from NOPE." Saturday Re-
view 55:69+, 6/3/72.
D192 Varnado, S. L. "Fear Fans Out." National Review

26:482+, 4/26/74.

D193 Vianney, Gina. "The Missing Link." Nursing Mirror
and Midwives Journal 130:50. 2/6/70.

D194 Wallace, Clare Marc. "A Change Is as God as..."
Nursing Times 66:94, 1/15/70.

D195 _____. "Eyes Right. Nursing Mirror and Midwives
Journal 134:37, 2/25/72.

D196 _____. "Theatre." Nursing Times 65:989, 7/31/69.

D197 Weithorn, Corinne J. and Brody, Elaine M. "Games
Professionals Play: Publishmanship or the Paper
Parlay." Gerontologist 8:284-6, Winter 1968.

Whitlock, R. SEE: Bentley, C.

D198 Williams, George. "Rabbits and the Grass: a Fable
for These Times." Christian Century 86:1453-4,
11/12/69.

D199 Williamson, Dereck. "Driving You to Drink: Devices
to Keep the Drunken Driver Off the Road." Saturday
Review 54:4, 12/25/71.

D200 _____. "If You Turn on the Heat, I'll Start the Air
Conditioner." Saturday Review 55:4, 5/13/72.

D201 _____. "Needle Is a Needle." Saturday Review 55:
6-7, 1/29/72.

D202 Wilson, David L. "A Poem to Be Read over Warm
Broth, while Waiting for Something to Develop."
Molecular and Cellular Biochemistry 2:105, 11/15/73.

D203 Zinsser, William Knowlton. "Nude Scene: [BLIP] Is
Beautiful." Life 67:16B, 8/8/69.

HOME AND FAMILY

E1　　Adler, Bill. "Dear Baby-Sitter; Last-Minute Instruc-
　　　tions." Good Housekeeping 168:122-3, 3/69.

E2　　Ayer, LaNeil. "We Did It: A Moat, Waterfall and
　　　Bridge in My Living Room." House Beautiful 113:
　　　24+, 4/71.

E3　　Baker, Russell. "Life's Precious Moments (Winter Di-
　　　vision)." Reader's Digest 97:35-6, 12/70.

E4　　　　　　. "Negative Thinking: Family Snapshots."
　　　New York Times Magazine p. 6, 7/14/74.

E5　　　　　　. "We're Rotten, Laura, Rotten to the Core."
　　　Life 66:18D, 2/21/69.

E6　　Barrett, Peter. "My Wife the Computer." Reader's
　　　Digest 93:117-18, 8/68.

E7　　Bolton, Thomas. "I Thought We'd Take the Din Out of
　　　Dinner." Reader's Digest 102:157-9+, 1/73.

E8　　　　　　. "Little Surprise for the Girls." Reader's
　　　Digest 100:90-3, 1/72.

E9　　Bombeck, Erma. "Four Faces of Erma." Today's
　　　Health 49:30-3, 8/71.

E10　　　　　　. "Gardening against the Odds." Good House-
　　　keeping 176:42+, 5/73.

E11　　　　　　. "How Not to Go Down the Drain." Good
　　　Housekeeping 178:42+, 1/74.

E12　　　　　　. "It's a Dog's Life." Good Housekeeping
　　　174:44+, 1/72.

E13　　　　　　. "Laughing through the Rites, and Wrongs,
　　　of Spring." Today's Health 51:52-3, 5/73.

E14　　　　　　. "Moving Made Easy." Good Housekeeping
　　　173:80+, 9/71.

E15　　　　　　. "Pity the Child Whose Parents Are With It";
　　　excerpt from Just Wait till You Have Children of
　　　Your Own. Today's Health 50:38-9, 2/72.

E16　　　　　　. "Pleasures (and Pitfalls) of Vacationing at
　　　Home." Good Housekeeping 177:64+, 7/73.

E17 _____, and Keane, Bil. "Revenge of Erma Bom-
     beck"; excerpt from Just Wait till You Have Chil-
     dren of Your Own. McCall's 98:24+, 8/71.
E18 Bridges, Annetta Hereford. "Hello, My Children,
     Good-By." Reader's Digest 99:157-60, 10/71.
E19 _____. "Where Did the Years All Fly?" PTA
     Magazine 66:14-6, 10/71.
E20 Briggs, Helen. "Encyclopedia Behind the Eggs."
     House Beautiful 113:76, 10/71.
E21 Bruce, Jeannette. "Slave to a Shah; Obedience Schools
     for Dogs." Sports Illustrated 30:86-92+, 5/5/69.
E22 Chadwick, Hal. "Last Resort; Vacation at Home."
     Today's Health 49:50-2, 5/71.
E23 Colen, Bruce David. "Calling in the Pros." House
     Beautiful 114:57, 11/72.
E24 Collier, James Lincoln. "How to Do Battle with
     Grownups." Reader's Digest 104:128-31, 5/74.
E25 Davis, Johanna. "Mastering Cooking Classes; Attend-
     ing Simone Beck Classes." Life 70:10-11, 2/19/71.
E26 Durrell, Gerald. "What Do You Mean, Too Hot?" ex-
     cerpt from A Bevy of Beasts. House & Garden 143:
     160+, 5/73.
E27 Engel, Kathleen Sanders. "If You Can Build a Box
     You've Got It Made." Better Homes & Gardens 52:
     42+, 10/74.
E28 Ferris, John. "Arf, Arf, and a Hearty Woof." Satur-
     day Review 54:6, 6/12/71.
E29 _____. "Ironing." Saturday Review 53:12+, 11/21/
     70.
E30 Ferris, Tim. "Motor Home Movies; or, Trouble in
     Paradise." Motor Trend 25:102, 3/73.
E31 Ford, Corey. "Trouble with Husbands; Fishing Widows."
     Field & Stream 74:6+, 9/69.
E32 Frances, Evan and Smith, Robert Paul. "Come Out
     and Play." Ladies' Home Journal 89:74+, 7/72.
E33 Friedrich, Otto. "Of Mice and Mice." McCall's 101:
     38+, 11/73.
E34 Good Housekeeping. "Understanding Those New Furni-
     ture Labels." Good Housekeeping 179:158, 8/74.
E35 Hamblin, Dora Jane. "Morning Glories and Alien
     Corn." Life 73:22, 9/8/72.
E36 Harnett, Ellen. "Mother-of-the-Gardener: What It
     Takes to Succeed." House Beautiful 113:30+, 3/71.
E37 Heath, Aloise Buckley. "Heath Christmas Carol Pro-
     gram." National Review 25:24-6, 1/5/73.
E38 _____. "Trapp Family Christmas." National Re-
     view 21:1317-19, 12/30/69.

E39 Hever, Robert. "Who Says a Man Can't Iron?" Good
       Housekeeping 173:42+, 8/71.
E40 Hochstein, Rollie. "My Husband, the String-Saver."
       Good Housekeeping 167:44+, 8/68.
E41 Johnson, Les. "Day My Son Grew a Foot." Good
       Housekeeping 168:34+, 6/69.
       Keane, Bil. SEE: Bombeck, Erma.
E42 Kerr, Jean. "Children's Hour after Hour after Hour."
       Ladies' Home Journal 85:72-3+, 8/68.
E43 _____. "How Wives Drive Husbands Crazy"; ex-
       cerpt from Penny Candy. Reader's Digest 97:85-7,
       12/70.
E44 _____. "Marriage: Unsafe at Any Speed."
       Reader's Digest 96:60-2, 5/70.
E45 Levenson, Sam. "Panic Button"; excerpt from In One
       Era and Out the Other. Ladies' Home Journal 90:
       48+, 12/73.
E46 Loughmiller, Isabell. "Confessions of a Trigger-Happy
       Housewife." Reader's Digest 94:84-6, 1/69.
E47 Lubold, Joyce Kissock. "I'd Rather Have a Man
       Handy than a Handy Man." Reader's Digest 92:183-
       4+, 6/68.
E48 McGahan, Mary. "Do It Yourself Grandmother."
       Harvest Years 8:2, 10/68.
E49 Micklo, Anne Marie. "Child's Christmas in Elizabeth,
       New Jersey." Senior Scholastic 101:30+, 12/11/72.
E50 Morton, Marcia. "Elderly Primipara, That's Me!"
       McCall's 97:92+, 10/69.
E51 O'Donnell, Richard W. "How to Assemble a Christ-
       mas Toy." Saturday Review 53:4+, 12/5/70.
E52 Park, W. B. "Ted Straight: Man on the Way Up."
       Look 35:48-9, 1/26/71.
E53 Rosten, Leo. "Happiest Couple in the World." Sat-
       urday Review World 1:36-7, 10/9/73.
E54 _____. "How to Tell Your Child about Sex." Look
       22:26, 10/15/68.
E55 Shane, Dorothy. "Over the River and Through the
       Woods." Harvest Years 9:29, 12/69.
E56 Skurzynski, Gloria. "Growing Pains." Good House-
       keeping 169:274D, 11/69.
E57 Smith, Frank Kingston. "Wife Problem." Flying 86:
       124, 5/70.
E58 Smith, Horace C., pseud. "Annual Report, Horace C.
       Smith Family, Inc." Changing Times 26:24, 1/72.
       Smith, Robert Paul. SEE: Frances, Evan.
E59 Sparks, Fred. "We Bathed by Candlelight." Mc-
       Call's 96:67+, 8/69.

E60 Stanton, Will. "Operation Easter Bunny." Reader's
     Digest 100:189-92, 4/72.
E61 _____. "Reaping Fatherhood's Rewards at Fifty."
     McCall's 97:50, 6/70.
E62 Trillin, Calvin. "Gourmet of the Golden Browns:
     French Fried Potatoes." Life 71:14, 8/27/71.
E63 Trotta, Geri. "Bon Voyage, But Don't Tell the Cat."
     House Beautiful 111:189, 10/69.
E64 Tupper, Margo. "Has Anybody Seen My Hammer?"
     Good Housekeeping 169:48+, 8/69.
E65 Venie, Hildegard. "Grandma Venie Gets the Works."
     Harvest Years 9:25, 2/69.
E66 Weinstein, Grace W. "Home Wasn't Rebuilt in a Day."
     House Beautiful 114:148, 2/72.
E67 Williamson, Dereck. "Goodbye, Old Paint." Saturday
     Review 55:67-8, 8/12/72.
E68 _____. "So You Want the Right Tool for the Job?"
     excerpt from The Complete Book of Pitfalls.
     Reader's Digest 98:148-50, 3/71.
E69 _____. "Spring Hangup"; excerpt from The Com-
     plete Book of Pitfalls. Saturday Review 54:6+,
     5/15/71.
E70 Worthington, Robin. "Try the Orange-Peel Approach."
     Reader's Digest 103:77+, 10/73.
E71 Zinsser, William Knowlton. "How to Get to Our
     House." Life 73:20, 11/8/72.

SECTION F:

LANGUAGE, LITERATURE
MASS MEDIA AND PUBLISHING

F1   Ace, Goodman. "Doing What Comes Fatuously." Saturday Review 54:6, 5/22/71.

F2   _____. "Equal and Equal = Nothing." Saturday Review 51:3, 1/20/68.

F3   _____. "Letter Writer." Saturday Review 55:5, 3/18/72.

F4   _____. "Polls." Saturday Review 55:4, 1/22/72.

F5   Aeschbacher, Jill. "It's Not Elves Exactly." College Composition and Communication 24:240-6, 10/73.

F6   American Heritage. "Through History with the Times: Headlines for Historical Incidents." American Heritage 22:112, 2/71.

F7   Amis, Kingsley and Conquest, Robert. "Short Educational Dictionary." New York Times Magazine p. 4+, 1/10/71.

F8   Angell, Roger. "How They Brought the Bad News from Ghent (N. Y.) to Aix (Kans.)." New Yorker 45:24-7, 1/3/70.

F9   _____. "Life in These Now United States." New Yorker 45:34-6, 3/15/69.

F10 Arlen, Michael J. "Air: Sunday." New Yorker 44:143-6+, 3/16/68.

F11 Armour, Richard. "Be Good to Your Authors." Publishers' Weekly 200:23, 8/9/71.

F12 Armstrong, David. "The Harassed TV Composer." World of Music 12:37-44 n. 4, 1970.

F13 Aurthur, Robert Alan. "Hanging Out: New Program Called 'Execution'." Esquire 82:24+, 7/74.

F14 Baker, Russell. "Slim Like a Butterfly." New York Times Magazine p. 6, 6/24/73.

F15 Barthelme, Donald. "Newsletter." New Yorker 46:23, 7/11/70.

F16 Barts, Fredrica K. "Immodest Proposal: Sanitary

Plan for Displacing Obscene Literature." English
Journal 59:43, 1/70.

F17 Bennett, Margaret, pseud. "Acceptance of the Month
Club." Publishers' Weekly 198:22-3, 12/7/70.

F18 _____. "Book Is Born." Publishers' Weekly 204:
36-7, 10/1/73.

F19 _____. "Rent-a-Script Caper." Publishers' Weekly 200:40, 8/2/71.

F20 Berger, Thomas. "Films." Esquire 78:70+, 7/72;
32, 8/72.

F21 Berlitz, Charles F. "Inscrutable Idioms of Dr. Yee."
Horizon 16:112, Autumn 1974.

F22 Bigg, Samuel. "Newspaper Fare." Journal of the
American Medical Association 204:407, 4/29/68.

F23 Bombeck, Erma. "Diary of a Sports Widow: A Year-
Long Log of TV-Watching by My Sports-Addict Husband." Good Housekeeping 175:66+, 9/72.

F24 Brien, Alan. "Greatest Story Never Told." Holiday
44:6-9, 8/68.

F25 Brooks, Albert. "Albert Brooks' Famous School for
Comedians." Esquire 75:89-94, 2/71.

F26 Brooks, Colleen. "Post Pastoral." New Yorker 44:
28-9, 6/1/68.

F27 Brown, Jeff. "High Art at Pike's Peak." Saturday
Evening Post 241:80-1, 3/23/68.

F28 Buckley, William Frank, Jr. "National Review Papers." National Review 23:850, 8/10/71.

F29 Cantwell, Mary and Gross, Amy. "WFEM Papers;
Soap Opera Script." Mademoiselle 77:200-1+, 5/73.

F30 Capote, Truman. "Blind Items; Society Gossip Col-
umns." Ladies' Home Journal 91:81+, 1/74.

F31 Christian Century. "More Functional Than Muzak."
Christian Century 88:639, 5/19/71.

F32 _____. "Pupwsss Poll." Christian Century 86:601,
4/23/69.

F33 _____. "Strike That Neologism!" Christian Century 86:793, 6/4/69.

F34 _____. "Vietnam Vocabulary: Terms Suitable for
Various Groups." Christian Century 88:87, 1/20/71.

F35 Chute, B. J. "End of It All; a Modern Fable."
Writer 82:15-18, 1/69.

F36 Ciardi, John. "Gold Fever." Saturday Review 54:10+,
2/13/71.

F37 Conger, Lesley. "This Very Moment." Writer 86:8,
1/73.

Conquest, Robert. SEE: Amis, Kingsley.

F38 Cowell, Jack and Jeanes, William. "Crisis Classifieds;

Possible Advertising of Goods and Services during
Gasoline Shortage." Car and Driver 19:69-71, 6/74.

F39   Craig, Jonah. "Fleas in Bed." From "The Tinker of
Turvey," 1630. Playboy 20:143+, 8/73.

F40   DeMott, Benjamin. "How Existential Can You Get?"
New York Times Magazine p. 4+, 3/23/69.

F41   Draughton, Ralph. "Ladies' Aid." An Alabama Tale
from "The Story of Selma." Playboy 20:155, 10/73.

F42   Ellis, H. F. "Books from the Wood." New Yorker 44:
81-3, 1/18/69.

F43   _____. "Without Whose Unfailing Encouragement."
New Yorker 45:24-5, 8/23/69.

F44   Esquire. "Bs: The Liberation of Olive Oyl." Esquire
78:219-26, 12/72.

F45   _____. "Few Words with the Masked Poet." Esquire 78:148-9+, 11/72.

F46   _____. "Peephole Weekly." Esquire 82:151-8,
12/74.

F47   _____. "Who Says a Good Newspaper Has to Be
Dull?" Esquire 72:200-8, 12/69.

F48   Ferris, John. "Press Conference." Saturday Review
53:4, 9/5/70.

F49   Fitch, Robert E. "Dictionary of Contemporary Delusions." Christian Century 86:377-8, 3/19/69.

F50   Francis, Arlene. "Memorable Minutes on 'What's My
Line?'" McCall's 96:88-9, 3/69.

F51   Freeman, David. "Media Fable; Personal Ads." New
York Times Magazine p. 22+, 12/10/72.

F52   Furth, Margo. "Word Game: On Becoming and Unbe-
coming a Syndicated Columnist." Critic 32:46-9,
3/74.

F53   Gerhardt, Lillian N. "Up for Discussion: a Modest
Proposal for the Very First Worst Children's Book
Aware Ever." Library Journal 96:1136-7, 3/15/71.

F54   _____. "Up for Discussion: Finn Pin Picked and
Budd Button Popped." Library Journal 96:1525, 4/
15/71.

F55   _____. "Up for Discussion: the Second Annual
Finn and Budd Awards." Library Journal 97:1622,
4/15/72.

F56   Gill, Jerry H. "Publish and Perish!" Christian Century 85:1206+, 9/25/68.

F57   Gold, Victor. "Gag Rule: Radio and Television Comedians as Presidential Speech Writers." National
Review 21:680, 7/15/69.

F58   _____. "Obscenity Gap." National Review 21:597,
6/17/69.

F59   Goldberg, Louis. "Faking It." <u>Ramparts</u> 6:59-62, 3/ 68.

F60   Gooch, Bryan N. S. and Westermark, Tory. "Poet and Poem: an Approach to Genius." <u>English Journal</u> 60: 465-8, 4/71.

F61   <u>Good Housekeeping</u>. "And Now a Few Words from Our Sponsor." <u>Good Housekeeping</u> 177:90-1+, 8/73.

F62   Gordon, George N. "Elimination of Reading; a Status Report." <u>Library Journal</u> 93:1729-32, 4/15/68; <u>School Library Journal</u> 15:57-60,4/68.

F63   Gough, Marion. "Travel; a Little Language Is a Dangerous Thing." <u>House Beautiful</u> 113:20+, 4/71.

     Gross, Amy. SEE: Cantwell, Mary.

F64   Halliday, E. M. "Backward Look at the New Politics; G. Washington's Preparation for a Television Appearance." <u>American Heritage</u> 19:112, 10/68.

F65   Handelsman, J. B. "Fables." <u>New Yorker</u> 49:40-1, 9/17/73.

F66   Hazelton, Nika Standen. "Winners! Results of Contest in Matching the Titles of Familiar Books to Familiar Persons." <u>National Review</u> 23:314+, 3/23/71.

F67   _____. "Writer's Reluctance." <u>National Review</u> 20: 504+, 5/21/68.

F68   Henderson, Bill. "My Great American Novel." <u>Chicago Review</u> 26 no. 1:52-64, 1974.

F69   Herndon, James. "Riders of the Silver Screen"; excerpt from <u>How to Survive in Your Native Land</u>. <u>Reader's Digest</u> 100:157-60, 6/72.

F70   Hoffman, Charles G. "In the Beginning." <u>College Composition and Communication</u> 23:406-9, 12/72.

F71   Horne, David. "How Did Amanda Get into This?" <u>Publishers' Weekly</u> 199:41, 1/11/71.

F72   Hutchinson, Larry. "Flash! Famous Novelist OD's on Coffee!" <u>Senior Scholastic</u> 98:36, 5/17/71.

     Jeanes, William. SEE: Cowell, Jack

F73   Jenkins, Russ. "Watch for These Birds." <u>Writer's Digest</u> 50:52-3, 6/70.

F74   Johnson, Valdon L. "Semantics and Dental Care." <u>North American Review</u> 7:79-80, Summer 1970.

F75   Kanfer, Stefan. "Is There Intelligent Life on Commercials?" <u>Time</u> 101:73, 4/16/73; <u>Reader's Digest</u> 103: 103:229-30, 10/73.

F76   Keillor, Garrison. "Around the Horne." <u>New Yorker</u> 50:33-4, 9/30/74.

F77   _____. "Found Paradise." <u>New Yorker</u> 47:32-3, 9/18/71.

F78   _____. "Plainfolks." <u>New Yorker</u> 50:44-6, 11/4/74.

F79   Lewin, Ralph A. "Pollution Is a Dirty Word." Nature
      231:65, 5/7/71.

F80   Life. Parting Shots: "Films that Will Offend Nobody."
      Life 70:62A-62B, 4/2/71.

F81   Lindsay, Cynthia. "Lexicon of International Small
      Talk." Harper's Bazaar 102:68-70, 12/68.

F82   Love, Harold. "Satirised Characters in 'Poeta de Tris-
      tibus'." Philological Quarterly 47:547-62, 10/68.

F83   Mackin, Tom. "Shakespeare as TV Critic." Clearing
      House 43:188-9, 11/68.

F84   Mahieu, Robert. "Monk Who Wouldn't Lie Down."
      From "Le Moine Segretain," a Twelfth Century
      French Fabliau. Playboy 20:226+, 12/73.

F85   Marcuse, Kenneth. "Cat 'o Nine Tales." From an
      Indonesian Folk Tale. Playboy 20:145, 7/73.

F86   Mathewson, Joseph. "Miss Buttonworth Wed to Fam-
      ily's Relief; Society Page and Coverage of Weddings."
      Look 35:9, 8/24/71.

F87   McNeil, Lily. "That Cosmopolitan Girl." New Yorker
      49:26-7, 7/16/73.

F88   Meehan, Thomas. "Cruise Director on the Titanic;
      Art Buchwald's Column." New York Times Maga-
      zine p.10-11+, 1/2/72.

F89   _____. "If You're Still Curious, Here Are Advance
      Reviews of Three Important Upcoming Movies (rating
      Z)." New York Times Magazine p.12-13, 6/29/69.

F90   Metcalf, Paul. "Big Charles: a Gesture towards Re-
      constitution." Prose no.8:163-77, Spring 1974.

F91   Middlebrook, Jonathan. "Television as the Medium of
      Contempt." Ramparts 7:56+, 4/69.

F92   Middleton, Thomas H. "Divine Dizziness." Saturday
      Review World 1:90, 9/11/73.

F93   Morris, Donald R. "Matter of Procedure." Reporter
      38:43-5, 2/22/68.

F94   Morrison, Joseph L. "View of the Moon from the Sun;
      1835." American Heritage 20:80-2, 4/69.

F95   Moss, Howard. "Instant Lives." Saturday Review 55:
      37, 9/9/72.

F96   Nathan, Simon. "I Am a Press Photographer, I Am,
      I Am, I Am." Popular Photography 73:52+, 11/73.

F97   _____. "It's Hard to Shoot a Bank in London."
      Popular Photography 64:70+, 5/69.

F98   _____. "Not Included Here: What the Los Angeles
      Police Didn't Do for Me." Popular Photography 70:
      44+, 4/72.

F99   _____. Simon Says: "They Don't Make News Pho-
      tographers Like They Used To. .." Modern Photog-

raphy 32:50+, 6/68.

F100 National Review. "Brinkley-Vanocur-Mudd-Reynolds
     Conspiracy; ed. by Walter Cronkite (As Told to Wil-
     liam Gavin)." National Review 23:824, 7/27/71.

F101 _____. "Day in the Life; Believer in All He Reads
     and Hears." National Review 22:933, 9/8/70.

F102 _____. "Secret Papers They Didn't Publish; Docu-
     ments Leaked to National Review." National Review
     23:798-811, 7/27/71; Discussion, 23:904, 915-8,
     975-6, 8/24 - 9/10/71.

F103 Navasky, Victor S. "Word Game." New York Times
     Magazine p. 14+, 2/9/69; Discussion, p. 6+, 3/9/69.

F104 New Republic. TRB from Washington: "Chitchat."
     New Republic 164:6, 4/3/71.

F105 New Yorker. "Lovborg's Women Considered." New
     Yorker 50:44-5, 10/28/74.

F106 Newman, Harold. "Death of the Maitre d'; or, Never
     End a Word with a Preposition." Saturday Review
     55:6-7, 2/26/72.

F107 Nichols, Olivia. "Keats and English 1013." College
     English 35:50-1, 10/73.

F108 Nordell, Roderick. "Like, I Mean, You Know, Right?"
     Reader's Digest 101:57-8, 9/72.

F109 O'Donnell, Richard W. "Till It Be Morrow; Future
     Goodnights from John Chancellor, Frank McGee,
     David Brinkley and NBC News." New Yorker 46:29,
     7/4/70.

F110 O'Toole, William. "Spiro and the Buchwald Blues."
     Commonweal 93:465, 2/12/71.

F111 Publishers' Weekly. "Letter to an Unknown (and Likely
     to Remain So) Author." Publishers' Weekly 198:44,
     10/26/70.

F112 Robinson, Sally. "What Should Parents See?" Seven-
     teen 28:42+, 1/69.

F113 Rolling Stone. "Special Issue of 'The Midnite Rambler'
     (Spoof on Current News)." Rolling Stone 152:insert,
     1/17/74.

F114 Rosenberg, Bernard. "Dictionary for the Disenchanted."
     Harper's 241:93-5, 11/70.

F115 Rosten, Leo. "Well, I'll Be Damned!" Look 34:16,
     2/10/70.

F116 Rummerfield, Philip S. "When I'm Put in Charge of
     Cleaning Up the American Version of the English
     Language." Health Physics 24:587-8, 5/73.

F117 Savage, Thomas. "Sir: If You Wish Us to Consider
     Further Your Manuscript of Goldilocks and the Three
     Bears..." Esquire 72:145+, 10/69.

F118 Schoenstein, Ralph. "We Interrupt This Way of Life
      ..." Saturday Evening Post 246:48+, 1/74.
F119 Sedulus, pseud. "1983." New Republic 166:23-4, 3/
      4/72.
F120 Shakespeare, Francis. "Oh, That Danish Blue!" National Review 23:192+, 2/23/71.
F121 Simoni, Anna E. C. "Shape of Things to Come?
      Mechanization in the Printing Industry." Book Collector 20:197-201, Summer 1971.
F122 Slavkin, Victor. "Tattooed Poem... Flesh and Blood
      Can't Bear It." Atlas 17:40, 3/69.
F123 Sorel, Edward. "Sorel's Unfamiliar Quotations." Atlantic Monthly 221:50-1, 5/68; 65, 6/68; 222:47,
      7/68; 84, 9/68; 77, 10/68.
F124 Steensma, Robert C. "Advanced Placement Student Explicates Fleas." English Journal 57:580, 4/68.
F125 Stein, Herbert. "My Turn: News Magazines' Personalization of Inflation." Newsweek 84:11, 7/29/74.
F126 Steinfels, Peter. "Books for Your Stocking." Commonweal 99:334, 12/28/73.
F127 _____. "Events Beyond My Control"; Letter to the
      Editor. Commonweal 99:287, 12/14/73.
F128 Stimson, William. "Decline of Humor." Saturday Review 55:4, 4/15/72.
F129 Taylor, Leon. "Teen-Age DJ." Saturday Review Education 1:12-13, 4/73.
F130 Tilney, Philip. "Potter and the Widow." From a Bulgarian Folk Tale. Playboy 20:161, 11/73.
F131 Trahey, Jane. "Confessions of a Movie Nut." McCall's 99:22+, 4/72.
F132 Trillin, Calvin. "Adventures of Roxanne: Notes on a
      Sensuous Woman." Life 69:12, 11/27/70.
F133 Tullius, F. P. "Ninety-Nine Years Is Not Forever."
      New Yorker 46:20-1, 7/19/69.
F134 Udell, Gerald. "On First Looking Into Chomsky's
      Halle; an Anti-Establishment Deviationist-Reactionary
      206-Line Sonnet in Free Verse." American Speech
      45:91-7, Spring-Summer 1970.
F135 Van Dyk, Howard. "Maximizing the Wheelbarrow; Interpreting W. C. Williams' 'The Red Wheelbarrow'."
      English Journal 61:510-2, 4/72.
      Westermark, Tory. SEE: Gooch, Bryan N. S.
F136 Wield, P. Jeffrey. "Hamlet and Claudius $\longrightarrow$ HCl +
      Energy"; with Reply by A. Bing. Chemistry 46:26-
      8, 4/73.
F137 Williams, Martin. "Open Letters." National Review
      23:1315, 11/19/71.

F138 Wilson Library Bulletin. "Hugo Flesch Worst Seller
        List." Wilson Library Bulletin 45:779, 4/71.
F139 Writer's Digest. "Grandee Land; the Game of Publish-
        ing." Writer's Digest 53:26-7, 11/73.
F140 _____. "Possession of Doriane Moore." Writer's
        Digest 53:28-31, 9/73.
F141 Zimmerman, Paul D. "No Movies Like These."
        Newsweek 82:122+, 9/24/73.
F142 Zinsser, William Knowlton. "Biggest Thing Since..."
        Life 65:10, 10/25/68.
F143 _____. "For Clear Expression: Try Words: the
        Interrobang." Life 65:24, 11/15/68.
F144 _____. "Let's Have a Symbol to Protect Pop; the
        New Movie Ratings." Life 66:11, 2/7/69.

SECTION G:

LAW AND CRIMINOLOGY

G1   Ace, Goodman. "Sprained Ankle." Saturday Review
       World 1:12, 12/4/73.
G2   Allen, Woody. "Whore of Mensa." New Yorker 50:37-
       8, 12/16/74.
G3   Almand, Bond. "Bar Salad with Bench Dressing."
       Georgia State Bar Journal 7:75, 8/70.
G4   Alsop, Stewart. "Sam Ervin Show." Newsweek 81:100,
       4/2/73.
G5   Arkansas Law Review. "Legislative and Judicial Dyna-
       misms in Arkansas: Poisson vs. d'Avril." Arkan-
       sas Law Review 22:724, Winter 1969.
G6   Baker, Russell. 'Bent Liberal." New York Times
       Magazine p. 6, 9/15/74.
G7   _____. "Rap on Zeal." New York Times Magazine
       p. 6, 7/15/73.
G8   _____. "Throwing the Book at Him." New York
       Times Magazine p. 6, 3/10/74.
G9   _____. "Watergate Gag." New York Times Maga-
       zine p. 6, 6/10/73.
G10 Beatty, Jerome, Jr. "Dossier on Leonardo Michel-
       angelo." Esquire 75:184+, 6/71.
G11 Bittker, Boris I. "Case of the Fictitious Taxpayer;
       the Federal Taxpayer's Suit Twenty Years after Flast
       vs. Cohen (88 Supreme Court 1942)." "Case of the
       Real Taxpayer"; reply to Professor Bittker, by Ken-
       neth Culp Davis. University of Chicago Law Review
       36:364, Winter 1969.
G12 _____. "Tax Shelters for the Poor?" Taxes 51:68,
       2/73.
G13 Blum, Walter J. "Anthropological Notes on Federal Tax
       Men." Taxes 46:499, 8/68; University of Chicago
       Law School Record 17:11, Fall 1969.
G14 _____. "Is Estate Planning Still With It?" Taxes
       49:659, 11/71.

G15 _____. "Tax Trends and Tendencies Today."
    Taxes 52:466-70, 8/74.

G16 _____ and Pedrick, Willard H. "Reform School Ap-
    proach to Estate and Gift Tax Revision." Taxes
    51:81, 2/73.

G17 Botto, Louis. "Confessions of the World's Lousiest
    Spy." Look 35:76+, 10/19/71.

G18 Brien, Alan. "No Bond Me." New Statesman 79:691-
    2, 5/15/70.

G19 Brody, Burton F. "Son of the Speluncean Explorer."
    Iowa Law Review 55:1233, 6/70.

G20 Brumbaugh, Robert S. "Protection from One's Self:
    a Socratic Dialogue on Maycock vs. Martin (30 Conn
    L J No. 6, Aug. 6, 1968, P. 5)." Connecticut Bar
    Journal 42:465, 12/69.

G21 Burroughs, William Seward. "Playback from Eden to
    Watergate." Harper's 247:84-6+, 11/73.

G22 Chamberlin, Anne. "Letter from the CIA." Saturday
    Evening Post 241:36-7, 3/23/68.

G23 Christian Century. "Handy Aid to Racist Judges."
    Christian Century 87:223, 2/18/70.

G24 _____. "Lawful Disorder." Christian Century 88:
    963, 8/11/71.

G25 _____. "Of Prurient Interest." Christian Century
    86:1233, 9/24/69.

G26 Ciardi, John. "Confessions of a Circuit Rider." Sat-
    urday Review 51:7-8+, 8/31/68.

G27 Cotler, Gordon. "Top Secret, Get Your Advance Copy
    Today." New Yorker 44:38-9, 4/6/68.

G28 Craig, George R. "Irreverent Verse." Duquesne Law
    Review 7:549, Summer 1969.

G29 Desmond, Charles S. "May It Please the Committee."
    Oklahoma Bar Association Journal 39:1177, 6/29/68.

G30 Duquesne Law Review. "Mackensworth vs. American
    Trading Transp. Co. 367 F Supp 373." Duquesne
    Law Review 12:717-21, Spring 1974.

G31 Esquire. "Havana Survival Kit." Esquire 71:139-41,
    6/69.

G32 Fagan, Dennis. "An, All Things Considered, Not,
    Realistically Speaking, Immodest Proposal." Na-
    tional Review 23:1115, 10/8/71.

G33 Fillmore, W. P. "Lighter Side of the Law." Mani-
    toba Bar News 39:114-23, 8/73.

G34 Fisher, Jacob. "Human Drama in Death and Taxes."
    Trusts and Estates 110:727, 9/71.

G35 Gardner, Woodford L., Jr. "With Pen-in-Hand and
    Tongue-in-Cheek." Kentucky Bar Journal 38:51-5+,
    10/74.

G36   Herbert, Alan Patrick. "Reign of Error." Chicago
         Bar Record 50:481, 6/69.
G37   Higginbotham, A. Leon, Jr. "Luncheon Address."
         American Bar Association Antitrust Law Journal 37:
         748, 1968.
G38   Journal of Legal Education. "Unhallowed Loathsome
         Perceptions." Journal of Legal Education 22:89,
         1969.
G39   Journal of the Beverly Hills Bar Association. "Perils
         of Paul or What to Do until the Lawyer Comes."
         Journal of the Beverly Hills Bar Association 2:30,
         11/68.
G40   Kanfer, Stefan. "Sherlock Holmes: the Case of the
         Strange Erasures"; Time Essay. Time 103:28-9,
         1/28/74.
G41   Laing, Alexander. "How I Didn't Shoot Eisenhower."
         New Republic 169:12-13, 8/18/73.
G42   Levinson, John O. "Of Game Plans, Powers, and
         Prerogatives." American Bar Association Journal
         59:373, 4/73.
G43   Lipez, Richard. "Coolest Man in the Room." Pro-
         gressive 38:50, 7/74.
G44   _____. "Everybody Does It." Progressive 38:66,
         11/74.
G45   _____. "Switchboard; Intragovernmental Bugging
         System." Progressive 38:22, 3/74.
G46   McKenna, Brian. "Judge and the Common Man."
         Modern Law Review 32:601, 11/69.
G47   Merriam, Eve. "From the Good Book." Nation 217:
         54-5, 7/16/73.
G48   Miller, Robert W. "Weary Dean." Federation of In-
         surance Counsel Quarterly 21:9, Spring 1971.
G49   Mortlock, Bill. "Every Poison Its Own Antidote."
         Alabama Law Review 21:513, Summer 1969.
G50   Murdoch, Converse and Wentz, Roy A. "Kidnap and
         Sky-Jack Victims' Tax Reform." Tax Law 25:141,
         Fall 1971.
G51   Murphey, Bob W. "That's My Opinion ... I Think."
         Nebraska Law Review 49:397, 1/70.
G52   Myers, Walter. "In the Matter of James Whitcomb
         Riley." Esquire 72:82+, 9/69.
G53   National Review. "Danger! Postman Coming!" Na-
         tional Review 25:134, 2/2/73.
G54   Navasky, Victor S. "Can You Top This? a New TV
         Show, and Other Bright Ideas for the F.B.I." New
         York Times Magazine p. 8-9+, 7/16/72.
G55   Newsweek. "Day That Will Live in Infamy; Scandal

Spinoffs." Newsweek 81:20-1, 6/25/73.

G56 Nichols, Peter M. "Getting into Michael's." Saturday
Review 55:20-1, 8/19/72.

G57 Oleck, Howard L. "Pompous Professions." Cleveland-
Marshall Law Review 18:276, 5/69.

G58 Pearce, Donn. "How to Take Off Your Pants while
Wearing Chains." Esquire 73:98-9, 2/70.

G59 Ramparts. "Gang War Erupts." Ramparts 12:6+, 8/
73.

G60 Roalfe, William R. "Humor in the Law Library."
Law Library Journal 64:37, 2/71.

G61 Rogin, Gilbert. "What John McGraw Said." Reporter
38:40-4, 6/13/68.

G62 Rubin, Asher. "Supreme Moment." Harvard Law
School Bulletin 23:13, 2/72.

G63 Sack, John. "Making Contact in Baltimore." Esquire
71:92-4+, 6/69.

G64 Sale, Kirkpatrick and Sorel, Edward. "Wadhwa Proposal: a Case for Legalized Bribery." Harper 249:
85-7, 11/74.

G65 Schuchman, Philip. "In Re: Social Science in the
Eastern District of Pennsylvania. United States Dis-
trict Court, Middle District, Nusquamia (Counsel
Have Asked to Remain Anonymous)." University of
Pittsburgh Law Review 32:463, Summer 1971.

G66 Schwartz, Lynne Sharon. "Theater." New Republic
170:20-1, 6/1/74.

G67 Serling, Robert. "Is It Safe to Fly?" Holiday 46:54-
5, 7/69.

G68 Sheppard, John W. "Stars in Their Crown or Thorns
in Our Sides?" Florida Bar Journal 47:223, 4/73.

Sorel, Edward. SEE: Sale, Kirkpatrick.

G69 Stanton, Will. "Just for Laughs: the Gingerbread
House Caper." Look 34:60, 9/8/70.

G70 Time. "Watergate Wit." Time 101:94, 6/25/73.

G71 Traynor, Roger J. "Chief Justice Warren's Fair Question." Georgetown Law Journal 58:1, 10/69.

G72 Trillin, Calvin. "Down the [Adjective Deleted] Road."
New Yorker 50:37, 5/13/74.

G73 _____. "Inquiring Demographer; This Week's Ques-
tion: How Do You Think Watergate Will Affect the
Energy Crisis?" with caricatures by E. Koren.
New Yorker 49:48-9, 12/17/73.

G74 Tullius, F. P. "Crimes You'll Never Read About."
New Yorker 49:40-1, 2/11/74.

G75 _____. "High Opinions." New Yorker 44:131-2,
6/8/68.

G76   Varnado, S. L.   "Block that Expletive!"   National Review 26:760+, 7/5/74.
G77   _____.   "Senator Furbelow Questions a CIA Agent." National Review 26:1297, 11/8/74.
G78   Waterman, Sterry R.   "Remarks."   Boston University Law Review 49:584, Summer 1969.
G79   Wax, Judith.   "Waterbury Tales"; poem.   Time 102: 20, 9/24/73; New Republic 169:24-5, 9/15/73; Newsweek 82:34, 9/24/73.
      Wentz, Roy A.   SEE: Murdoch, Converse.

LIBRARY SCIENCE

H1   A B Bookman's Weekly. "How to Order from This
      Catalogue." A B Bookman's Weekly 53:1985-7,
      5/13/74.

H2   American Libraries. "A. L. Hot Line; Late Breaking
      News from the Good Offices of American Libraries."
      American Libraries 3:365, 4/72.

H3   Anderson, Frank John. "On Getting Ahead in the Li-
      brary Profession." "Atlantic Provinces Library As-
      sociation Bulletin 32:105-8, 12/68.

H4   Atkinson, Frank. "Dear Readers: Library Eccentrics."
      New Library World 73:119, 10/71.

H5   _____. "Do Be Careful with Whom You Associate."
      New Library World 73:198, 1/72.

H6   _____. "Grass Roots: a Romantic Novel Set in a
      Public Library of Today." New Library World 73:
      369-70, 8/72.

H7   BCLA Reporter. "Children Appreciative of the Library
      Ladies." BCLA Reporter 17:11, 9/73.

H8   _____. "Librarian Makes Her Point." BCLA Re-
      porter 16:4+, 5/73.

H9   Beard, Henry. "Hummorhoids; the Big Slipcase." Na-
      tional Lampoon p.30+, 2/73.

H10 Beatty, Patricia and Beatty, John. "Stalking the Way-
      ward Query; Tribute to the Beleaguered but Dauntless
      Reference Librarian." American Libraries 4:141-4,
      3/73.

H11 Berry, John N. III et al. "LJ's Annual Awards." Li-
      brary Journal 96:4043, 12/15/71; 97:3945, 12/15/72;
      98:3591, 12/15/73; comment by Charles O'Halloran,
      99:318, 2/1/74.

H12 _____. "LJ's Non-Awards." Library Journal 95:
      4207, 12/15/70.

H13 Birley, Robert. "Meeting a Crisis: Patron Saints for
      Bibliophiles, Printers and Bookbinders." Book Col-

lector 23:187-93, Summer 1974.
H14   Blei, Norbert. "Phantom of the Library." American
      Libraries 2:367-9, 4/71.
H15   Brady, Simon. "Man-Machine Dialogue." LASIE 4:
      36-7, 11/73.
H16   British Columbia Library Quarterly. "What Now? The
      Voice of the Seventies." British Columbia Library
      Quarterly 27:31-3, Summer-Autumn 1973.
H17   Brodney, Kay. "Invocation." Wilson Library Bulletin
      45:777, 4/71.
H18   Burgess, Anthony, pseud. "What's All This Fuss about
      Libraries?" Library Journal 93:1114-15, 3/15/68.
H19   Butler, Patrick. "Catching Up with the Wig Lady."
      Wilson Library Bulletin 45:775, 4/71.
H20   Carter, John Mitchell. "Nightmares along the Talla-
      hatchie Bridge." Library Journal 95:2889, 9/15/70.
H21   Christ, John Michael. "Short Story; an Unusual Library
      Exhibit." Mountain Plains Library Association
      Quarterly 18:31-6, Summer 1973.
H22   Curley, Arthur. "Rags to Riches." Library Journal
      97:1405, 4/15/72.
H23   _____. "Rough Edges; Considering the Welfare of
      the Community." Library Journal 97:2817, 9/15/72;
      reply, S. H. Wolf, 97:3829-30, 12/1/72.
H24   _____. "Staff Communication." Library Journal
      97:2161, 6/15/72.
H25   _____. "Tale of Two Sectors: Private and Public."
      Library Journal 97:657, 2/15/72.
H26   Davies, John Howard. "Poor Jeanie; or, Where Are
      the Notes of Yesteryear?" Brio 5:9-10, n.2, Au-
      tumn 1968.
H27   Davinson, Donald Edward. "You Don't Say, Mr. Chair-
      man." New Library World 75:33-4, 2/74.
H28   DeCamp, Dot. "Smith/Jones." Library Journal 95:
      3451, 10/15/70. Reply, Paul M. Kasprzak, 96:
      902, 3/15/71.
H29   Doiron, Peter M. "Booktalk Time." Library Journal
      98:3613, 12/15/73.
H30   _____. "Oral History: SRRT." Library Journal
      98:3355, 11/15/73.
H31   Draganski, Donald. "Eulogies to Pigeons." RQ (ALA
      Reference Service Division) 10:212-13, Spring 1971.
H32   DuFrane, Gerard, pseud. "Administering Our State
      Library Agencies; an Application of Scientific Man-
      agement Principles to a Pivotal Institution." Amer-
      ican Libraries 1:23-6, 1/70.
H33   Dunne, Finley Peter. "Carnegie Libraries." Journal

of Library History 5:166-70, 4/70.
H34 Durnell, Jane. "Irrepressible Deceiver." Pacific
Northwest Library Association Quarterly 36:17-23,
10/71.
H35 Dykins, Jeanne. "Library Gallimaufry to Digest at
Leisure, Being a Comprehensive Guide to the Gentle
Art of Book Reviewing; with a Key to Book Selection,
Usage, Terminology, Footnotes, Foreign Phrases and
Various and Assorted Sundries of Library Life in the
Year of Melvil Dewey, 1972." Ohio Library Associa-
tion Bulletin 42:11-13, 10/72.
H36 Erlich, Martin. "He-Libes vs. Women's Lib." Un-
abashed Librarian No. 3:17-19, Spring 1972.
H37 Everson, Jean E. "Lolling It Up; Proposed New Divi-
sion: Little Old Lady Librarians of ALA"; letter to
the editor. American Libraries 2:1039, 11/71.
H38 Falby, Marikay. "Funny Thing Happened on the Way to
the Library." Canadian Library Journal 25:42-3,
7/68.
H39 Flanagan, Cathleen C. "Wandering through the British
Museum Catalogue." RQ (American Library Associ-
ation. Reference and Adult Services Division) 13:31-
4, Fall 1973.
H40 Frangie, James. "Droves of Academe; a Contemporary
Dialog." Learning Today 7:26-33, Winter 1974.
H41 Gahuvnik, Schroeder and Pourciau, L. J. "Placid
Puddle Rest Home; a Proposal." South Carolina Li-
brarian 13:14-15, 10/68.
H42 Gell, Marilyn T. "Cry Wolf"; letter. Library Journal
99:939-40, 4/1/74.
H43 Goldmann, W. E. "What Would Happen If the Students
Got Locked in with All Those Books?" California
School Libraries 42:5-7, Fall 1970.
H44 Gore, Daniel. "Alfred the Great and the Reserve
Book." American Libraries 3:405-8, 4/72; comment
by Philip G. Becker. Unabashed Librarian no. 4:18,
Summer 1972.
H45 _____. "Faculty Status for the Librarians at Arbuth-
not." American Libraries 2:283-95, 3/71; discus-
sion, 2:567-9, 683, 783, 785, 6-9/71.
H46 Gribbin, Lenore Sipes. "Results of a Study of the Fac-
tors Influential in the Selection of Cataloging as a
Career." Library Journal 93:2977, 9/1/68; comment
by S. Clay, Library Journal 93:3485, 10/1/68.
H47 Groom, Edwina and others. "Librarian's Life: Four
Sketches." Library Review 22:68-74, Summer 1969.
H48 Grotzinger, Laurel Ann and Noble, Valerie. "Anyone

Here for Libe-Gab?" Special Libraries Association.
Advertising and Marketing Division Bulletin 25:3,
11/68.

H49 Guy, Leonard C. "Nervous Depression." Assistant
Librarian 61:101-3, 5/68.

H50 Hake, Shirley Dean. "My Debt to a Fusty Musty Librarian." Montana Libraries 21:6-7, 10/67.

H51 Hale, Lucretia P. "Peterkin Papers; Excerpts." Wilson Library Bulletin 42:1014-15, 6/68.

H52 Hanson, Virginia. "And Don't Use the Encyclopedia!"
Utah Libraries 13:29-31, Fall, 1970.

H53 Haro, Robert Peter. "Professional Status; the Revolt
of the Nopros." Wilson Library Bulletin 44:555-6,
1/70.

H54 Heathorn, R. J. "Learn with BOOK." Antiquarian
Bookman 31:1182, 3/25/63;reprinted from Punch p.
712, 5/9/62. Same with title: "Ultimate Teaching
Machine." Harper's 226:52, 4/73.

H55 Heinz, John. "Self-Soaring Information System." Unabashed Librarian no. 5:16, Fall 1972.

H56 Hickey, Doralyn Joanne. "Advanced Referencemanship." RQ (ALA Reference Services Division) 7:93-
4, Winter 1967; Montana Libraries 21:19-20, 4/68.

H57 Hollander, Stephen. "Here We Go 'Round the Vannevar
Bush." Canadian Library Journal 27:28-9, 1/70.

H58 Hudgins, Barbara M. "Psychology Course for Librarians." A B Bookman's Weekly 41:2126-8, 6/3-
10, 1968; reprinted from Doorway, 1/68.

H59 Indexer. "Indexers Will Not Be Replaced by Computers." Indexer 9:33-4, 4/74.

H60 Jacobson, Betty. "Women's Work: a Job Description."
Library Journal 96:2596, 9/1/71.

H61 Johnson, C. "Games People Play." New Library
World 73:365-6, 8/72.

H62 Jones, Harold D. "Memo to the Building Committee."
Library Journal 96:1579, 5/1/71.

H63 Kesselman, Jeff. "Librarian vs. Publisher." Library
Journal 95:4221-4, 12/15/70.

H64 Kister, Kenneth F. "Wind in the Winchells: or, Mr.
Toad Goes to Library School." Library Journal 96:
1687, 5/15/71.

H65 Knudson, Rozanne. "Excerpts from a Censor's Rhetor-
ic." RQ (ALA Reference Services Division) 10:209-
11, Spring 1971.

H66 _____, and Zibas, Jan. "Censor's Horoscope."
American Libraries 2:180-5, 2/71.

H67 Library Journal. "Brooklyn Bibliodelics: Local Chil-

dren Interviewed Members of the Library Staff;
Quotes from the Children's Essays." Library Journal 93:2978-9, 9/1/68.

H68 _____. "Personnel Work at Irvine: Astrology and
a Chaplain." Library Journal 95:3233-4, 10/1/70.

H69 Lockett, Don. "Those Wide Open Spaces." New Library World 74:75-6, 4/73.

H70 Mahy, Margaret. "Short Story: the Librarian and the
Robbers." New Zealand Libraries 35:195-200, 6/72.

H71 Massman, Virgil F. "ENWACBUCL; a Librarian's
Dream." American Libraries 3:285-8, 3/72. Comment by D. J. Patten, 3:587-8, 6/72.

H72 McConnell, James Michael. "Overdue; Alex in Wonderland, a Library Fantasy." Wilson Library Bulletin
48:845-7, 6/74. Comment by Dorothy M. Broderick,
49:31-2, 9/74.

H73 Morris, Leslie R. "Why Not Both? a Dictionary Catalog and a Divided Catalog." Library Resources and
Technical Services 17:25-7, Winter 1973.

H74 Moses, Richard B. "CANACONDA?" Library Journal
96:915-7, 3/15/71.

H75 _____. "The Meeting." American Libraries 2:244-
5, 3/71.

H76 Mountain Plains Library Quarterly. "Short Story."
Mountain Plains Library Quarterly 18:14-16+, Spring
1973.

H77 Nelson, Eva. "Why We Hardly Have Any Picture Books
in the Children's Department Anymore; a Brief Fantasy." Top of the News 29:54-6, 11/72.

H78 New Library World. "Ex Cathedra: Aslib Chemical
Group Biennial Conference at Churchill College, Cam-
bridge." New Library World 74:125, 6/73.

H79 New Yorker. Notes and Comment: "Library of Human
Resources." New Yorker 50:43, 11/18/74.

Noble, Valerie. SEE: Grotzinger, Laurel Ann.

H80 North, John. "Valete Mrs. Finkleblintz." A B Bookman's Weekly 41:1267-8, 4/1-8, 1968; reprinted from
Doorway, 1/68.

H81 Nyren, Karl. "Hooper and the Very Rich." Library
Journal 95:2745, 9/1/70.

H82 _____. "Hooper Heads for Dallas." Library Journal 96:1337, 4/15/71.

H83 _____. "Hooper in Dallas." Library Journal 96:
1686, 5/15; 2059, 6/15/71.

H84 _____. "Hooper in Love." Library Journal 96:803,
3/1/71.

H85 _____. "Hooper Strikes Back: Revenge for Esquire

        Ad from American Motors." Library Journal 96:171,
        1/15/71.
H86 _____. "Spiro and the Goddess of Love." Library
        Journal 96:3098-9, 10/1/71.
H87 _____. "Spiro and the Recession." Library Journal
        96:2467, 8/71.
H88 Olofson, Shirley. "Kansas City Hop; or, How Novia
        Sprained Her Ankle at ALA and Found Her Footing";
        short play. ALA Bulletin 63:817-26, 6/69.
H89 Peele, David A. "Cataloging on the Wall." Wilson
        Library Bulletin 45:772-4, 4/71.
H90 _____. "Overdone: Dumping Your Thing and Con-
        verting Catalogers into Useful Members of Society in
        Four Steps." Wilson Library Bulletin 48:648-9,
        4/74.
H91 _____. "Was Melvil Dewey a Whig? Being a Post-
        humous Account by a No-Account." Wilson Library
        Bulletin 46:727-32, 4/72.
H92 Petru, William C. "United States Controls on the Ex-
        portation of Unclassified Technical Data: a Fabled
        Account." Special Libraries 60:596-600, 11/69.
H93 Pirnie, Jane. "Jane Pirnie's Puzzler." Wilson Li-
        brary Bulletin 45:778-9, 4/71. Solution, 45:831+,
        5/71.
H94 Plotnik, Arthur. "Modest Proposal." Library Journal
        98:1707-8, 5/15/73.
    Pourciau, L. J. SEE: Gahuvnik, Schroeder.
H95 Powers, Thomas H. "Book Selection Committees and
        Warped Libidos." Wilson Library Bulletin 46:756,
        4/72.
H96 Richardson, Bernard E. "Manly Art: Book Selection."
        Library Journal 96:446-9, 2/1/71.
H97 _____. "Quo Jure? Advertising for Suitable Li-
        brarian to Serve American Indians without Discrimi-
        nating." American Libraries 2:304-5, 3/71.
H98 _____. "Welcome to My Three-by-Five World."
        American Libraries 3:67-9, 1/72; reply, S. O.
        Lundberg, 3:226-7, 3/72.
H99 Roberts, Don. "Yippie Librarianship." American Li-
        braries 1:1046-51, 12/70.
H100 Rowe, Austin. "Load of British Rubbish." New Li-
        brary World 75:4-5, 1/74.
H101 Ruby, Homer V. "Funny Thing Happened on the Way
        to the Computer." Illinois Libraries 54:183-5, 3/72.
H102 Sable, Arnold P. "Libraries, Love, and the Pursuit
        of Happiness; Some Pleasantly Sentimental Recollec-
        tions for the Christmas Season." Wilson Library

Bulletin 47:343-52, 12/72.

H103 _____. "Library Birds I Have Known." RQ (ALA
Reference Services Division) 8:193-5, Spring 1969.

H104 Sagoff, Maurice. "Operation Shrink-Lit." Mademoiselle 66:155+, 4/68.

H105 Sexton, Peggy B. "Take Us to Your Readers; Interplanetary Outreach." Wilson Library Bulletin 46:
921-3, 6/72.

H106 Shaw, John Bennett. "Sub Librarians Scion of the
Baker Street Irregulars." Canadian Library Association Feliciter 14 no. 7-8-9 pt. 1:5, 3-4-5/69.

H107 Shields, Gerald R. Editor's Choice: "Confidential,
Confidential; Annual Report, Credence State University." American Libraries 2:1149, 12/71.

H108 _____. Editor's Choice: "Conversational Tidbits
for Next Library Cocktail Party." ALA Bulletin
63:1057, 9/69.

H109 _____. Editor's Choice: "Snippets from Library-
land Inspired by the Opening of a Florida Branch of
Fantasyland." American Libraries 2:1043, 11/71.

H110 _____. Editor's Choice: "A Story Told in the
Temple Ruins." American Libraries 2:581, 6/71.

H111 _____. "Sorry the Library-Line Is Busy!" Library
Journal 99:1105, 4/15/74.

H112 _____. "Take Two Ethics and Drink Lots of Liq-
uids." Library Journal 99:1781, 7/74.

H113 Smith, Elizabeth. "Hey, Miss!" Letter to the editor.
ALA Bulletin 63:429, 4/69.

H114 Stevens, Norman D. "Molesworth Institute Revisited."
ALA Bulletin 63:1275-7, 10/69.

H115 Stewart, Ben. " 'Librarians Are One of the Main By-
Products of Books' and Other Enlightening Fourth-
Grade Observations on You, the Librarian." Wilson
Library Bulletin 48:38-41, 9/73.

H116 Taylor, David C. "Down with Title Changes!" American Libraries 5:165, 4/74.

H117 Taylor, Larry D. "Extra! Great Literary Find."
Catholic Library World 44:269-73, 12/72.

H118 Terpsichore, pseud. "Midwinter Night's Bummer
Dream." American Libraries 2:23, 1/71.

H119 Vagianos, Louis. "Conversation with a Computer;
Problems Facing Librarians." Library Journal 98:
3608-11, 12/15/73.

H120 _____. "Scaling the Library Collection." Library
Journal 98:712-15, 3/1/73; discussion, 98:1737, 6/
1/73.

H121 Werkley, Caroline E. "A!L!A! A!L!A! Here We

Go! Rah! Rah! Rah! Conventions Past." <u>Library</u>
<u>Journal</u> 94:2421-4, 6/15/69.

H122 _____. "Odds and Ends; a Recommended Course
for Library Schools." <u>Library Review</u> 22:3-5,
Spring 1969.

H123 <u>Wilson Library Bulletin</u>. "Amerikan Libraries' News-
weak, April 1, 1974; News that Suits the Format."
<u>Wilson Library Bulletin</u> 48:641-7, 4/74.

H124 _____. "April Foolery." <u>Wilson Library Bulletin</u>
46:726-39, 4/72; 47:671-83, 4/73.

H125 _____. "Library Germule." <u>Wilson Library Bulle-</u>
<u>tin</u> 44:839-47, 4/70.

H126 Wooster, Harold. "Machina Versatilis; a Modern
Fable." <u>Library Journal</u> 94:725-7, 2/15/69.

H127 Wright, Keith C. "Assured Failure in Information Center Operations." <u>Journal of the American Society</u>
<u>for Information Science</u> 22:294-5, 7/71.

H128 Yates, J. Michael. "Realia; Short Story." <u>British</u>
<u>Columbia Library Quarterly</u> 36:35-64, 7/72.

Zibas, Jan. SEE: Knudson, Rozanne.

SECTION I:

MUSIC AND PERFORMING ARTS

I1   Allen, Woody. "Guide to Some of the Lesser Ballets."
     New Yorker 48:34-5, 10/28/72.
I2   Ameritus, P. "Child's Guide to Modern Music." Com-
     poser (London) n. 31:28-9, Spring 1969.
I3   Armstrong, David. "How to Win Contracts and Influ-
     ence Directors." Composer (London) n. 34:33-5,
     Winter 1969-70.
I4   Audio. "ZYX Phono Systems." Audio 57:69, 4/73.
I5   Auerbach, Arnold M. "Looey, Pride of the Brill Build-
     ing; Greatest Electronic Songwriter." Variety 249:
     150, 1/3/68.
I6   Baden, June M. "Confessions of a Church Organist."
     Journal of Church Music 15:18-19, 4/73.
I7   Bar-Illan, David. "Drop-In Night at the Electric Cir-
     cus." Saturday Review 52:72-3, 11/15/69.
I8   Barton, Clement A. "Happenings in the Music World."
     Woodwind World 9:16-17 n. 2; 18-19 n. 3, 1970.
I9   Bearfoot, Margaret E. "Reluctant Alto." Musical
     Opinion 94:183+, 1/71.
I10 Beckmesser, Frederick. "Grades Ad Parnassum
     (Rocky Pathway to Musical Knowledge)." Stereo
     Review 31:66-9, 8/73.
I11 Bergmann, W. "Twenty-Six Golden Rules for Ensemble
     Playing." American Recorder 13:76-7 n. 3, 1972.
I12 Black, S. "Programme Notes: 'Three Blind Mice'."
     Performing Right n. 50:11, 10/68.
I13 Boutillier, Mary. "Life in the Teaching Studio (as
     Seen through the Melting Brown Eyes of a Dachs-
     hund)." Music Journal 26:44-5, 6/68.
I14 Bowers, Faubion. "Where Are All Those Mad Hatters,
     Wild and Carefree, of the Past?" Opera News 33:
     9-12, 12/21/68.
I15 Boyd, Jack. "When the Slicks Reviewed the Half-Time
     Show." Music Journal 26:56-7, 1/68.

I16   Brickman, Marshall. "Up in Front, Please." New
       Yorker 49:46-7, 12/3/73.
I17   _____. "What, Another Legend?" New Yorker
       49:32-3, 5/19/73.
I18   Brudnoy, David. "Faith Triumphant." National Review
       26:706, 6/21/74.
I19   Butler, John Harrison. "Art in the Afterworld."
       Music Educators Journal 54:62-6+, 2/68.
I20   Caisse, George. "Hold the Forte." Music Journal 28:
       60, 6/70.
I21   Canby, Edward Tatnall. "Dr. Bowes' Amateur Hour."
       Audio 52:24, 3/68.
I22   Capella, Robert. "Here We Go Again...." Instrument-
       alist 27:22, 8/72.
I23   Carlton, Lilyn E. "How to Hold the Violin; Beginner's
       Trauma." Music Journal 26:32+, 5/68.
I24   Cazden, Norman. "The Second Note Is Free." Music
       Review 30:237-42, n.3, 1969.
I25   Chay, Marie. "Are They Married?" Opera News 33:
       6-7, 12/14/68.
I26   Choppen, Edward. "My First Opera." Music in Edu-
       cation 37:254-5 n.363, 1973.
I27   _____. "Not in Mournful Numbers (Metrication of
       Music)." Music in Education 36:76-7 n.354, 1972.
I28   Cone, Edward Toner. "Beethoven New-Born." Amer-
       ican Scholar 38:389-400, Summer 1969.
I29   Crowder, Louis. "The Great Chaminade Festival."
       Clavier 10:17-20 n.4, 1971.
I30   Culshaw, John. "Fragments from an Unwritten Auto-
       biography." High Fidelity and Musical America 23:
       55-8, 6/73.
I31   Custer, Arthur R. "I Hate Music! A Musician's Ad-
       vice to College Freshmen." American Music Teach-
       er 17:42-3, n.5, 1968.
I32   Daheim, David C. "... And Do Not Scratch Yourselves
       Onstage." Opera News 32:6-7, 3/30/68.
I33   Dawbarn, Bob. "Bob Dawbarn on the 'Underground'."
       Melody Maker 44:17, 5/17/69.
I34   De Cola, Felix. "G. B. Shaw--the Critic." Clavier 9:
       21 n.7, 1970.
I35   _____. "The Piano, Its Uses and Idiosyncrasies."
       Clavier 8:16-17, n.9, 1969.
I36   Derwent, Lavinia. "Opera Forever... and Ever."
       Music Journal 26:101+, 12/68.
I37   DeVinney, Richard. "There's More to Church Music
       than Meets the Ear." Journal of Church Music 14:
       2-5, 9/72.

I38   Docherty, G. M. "A Guardsman Remembers." Opera
      (Eng.) 24:22-7, 1/73.
I39   Doyle, Louis. "The Imaginary Muse (Translations in
      Bilingual Librettos)." Opera News 37:16, 4/14/73.
I40   Dutton, A. M. "Organs and Organists." Musical
      Opinion 91:677, 9/68.
I41   Elliott, J. "My Poppadam Tol' Me (Origin of Jazz)."
      Melody Maker 44:8, 6/7/69.
I42   Elliott, Kim Andrew. "The Drummer's Anguish."
      Music Journal 27:46+, 4/69.
I43   Epstein, Eugene V. "Enough of Stiffelto." Opera
      News 34:16, 2/14/70.
I44   Esquire. "Now, Sing 'Melancholy Baby'." Esquire
      71:158-9+, 5/69.
I45   Farkas, Andrew. "Welcome to the Club; Operagoers."
      Opera News 34:6-7, 2/21/70.
I46   Favia-Artsay, Aida. "Grace Notes." Hobbies 77:35-
      6+, 2/73.
I47   Ferris, John. "Disadvantaged Youth." Opera News
      34:13, 3/14/70.
I48   Fogel, Henry. "Discs that Should Never Have Been
      Released." High Fidelity and Musical America 23:
      32+, 10/73.
I49   Forssell, Anna Lisa. "Are Piano Lessons Worth It?"
      Music Journal 29:67-8, 2/71.
I50   Freedman, Roma Sachs. "Anecdotal Musicals."
      Music Journal 28:61+, 6/70.
I51   Friedman, Bruce Jay. "Let's Hear It for a Beautiful
      Guy." New Yorker 50:37-9, 4/8/74.
I52   Gilson, Estelle. "Up the Down La Scala (Humorous
      Use of Operatic Phrases for Communicating in
      Italy)." Opera Journal 6:29-31 n.1, 1973.
I53   Goldsmith, Harris. "Recordings Fit for a President?"
      High Fidelity and Musical America 23:84, 10/73.
I54   Goodfriend, James. "A Humorous Note." Stereo Re-
      view 26:52+, 3/71.
I55   Gray, Barbara Ann. "What If I'd Had to Carry My
      Organ? (Amused View of Concert Tours)." Tri-
      angle of Mu Phi Epsilon 67:16-17 n.2, 1973.
I56   Grosswirth, Marvin. "Mengelwaengler: 'Sixty-five
      Years on the Podium Is Enough.'" High Fidelity
      and Musical America 23:67, 1/73.
I57   Haber, Leo. "Keyboard Side, Please!" High Fidelity
      and Musical America 22:60-1, 1/72.
I58   _____. "Who Really Wrote Beethoven's Music?"
      High Fidelity and Musical America 22:57-9, 11/72.
I59   Herbert, Susan. "Ring of the Nibble-Ung." Opera

25:198-9, 296-7, 440-1, 3-5/74.

I60   Hershfield, Harry. "Living in the Past." Music Journal 26:38-40+, 4/68.

I61   Hinze, Ellsworth. "How's Your Piano? (Problems of
Tuners with their Clients)." Clavier 8:15 n.5, 1969.

I62   Horne, Elliot. "Playback." Down Beat 39:10, 5/25/72.

I63   Horner, Keith. "National Orchestral Festival." Musical Times 111:1106, 11/70.

I64   Howard, Colin P. "Decimalization of Music 1973
(Tongue-in-Cheek Proposal)." Royal College of Music
Magazine 68:50 n.2, 1972.

I65   Howard, Richard. "Child's Guerdon of Opera." Prose
no. 8:151-61, Spring 1974.

I66   Hughes, Donald. "Neo-Matins." Hymn Society of
Great Britain and Ireland 7:40-3 n.2, 1969.

I67   Industrial Engineering. "How to Be Efficient with Few-
er Violins." Industrial Engineering p.57, 2/69.

I68   Inwood, Paul. "The Crown of Jesus Hymnbook (Out-
of-Print Hymnal of 1864)." Church Music 3:14-17
n.20, 1973.

I69   Jack, Michael. "Munch while You Pray." Musical
Opinion 91:447, 5/68.

I70   _____. "What Can We Do with an Organ Pipe?"
Musical Opinion 95:251+, 2/72.

I71   Jackson, Richard H. "The Bibliography that Might
Have Been." Notes 27:458-60 n.3, 1971.

I72   Jacobs, Frank. "Musical Chairs (Interrelationships
between Composers of the Nineteenth Century)."
About the House 4:17-19 n.2, 1973.

I73   Journal of Church Music. "Dialogue between an Organist and a Parishioner." Journal of Church
Music 15:23+, 4/73.

I74   Kirton, Hilda. "Attics and Strads." Strad 84:299+,
9/73.

I75   Kissel, Leo. "Fiddles." Strad 83:511+, 2/73.

I76   Klaviter, J. B. "Through Eyes of the Uhts (Facetious
Look at Concert Touring)." Triangle of Mu Phi
Epsilon 67:17 n.2, 1973.

I77   Knight, Mark. "Sottanini e Violoncelli." Musical
Opinion 95:68-9, 11/71.

I78   Kraglund, John. "Applause." Opera Canada 10:12-13
no.1, 1969.

I79   Lamb, Elizabeth Searle. "Confessions of an Ex-Harpist." Music Journal 28:110, 3/70.

I80   Lees, Gene. "Modest Proposal (Narcotics and Music
Business)." High Fidelity and Musical America
20:116, 6/70 sec.1.

I81   Lentz, Daniel K. "Music Education." Composer (U.S.)
          1:150-3 n.3, 1969.
I82   Lester, Elenore. "Final Decline and Total Collapse of
          the American Avant-Garde." Esquire 71:142-3+,
          5/69.
I83   Levine, Mary. "The Year in Church Music (for Heav-
          en's Sake)." Music Journal 28:37, 7/70.
I84   Lewin, Robert. "Memorable Moments." Strad 82:
          197+, 9/71.
I85   _____. "Musings on Conductors." Strad 80:349+,
          12/69.
I86   Longmire, John. "Bax and John Ireland." Arnold Bax
          Society Bulletin n.6:99-101, 8/69.
I87   Lyall, Derek. "Fiddle-itis and Its Symptoms." Strad
          84:39+, 5/73.
I88   Lyons, Leonard. "Backstage; Sardi's." Holiday 43:
          66-71, 5/68.
I89   Macdonald, Hugh. "Death of Alkan." Musical Times
          114:25, 1/73.
I90   Mano, D. Keith. "Culture in Middletown." National
          Review 26:1414, 12/6/74.
I91   Marcato, B. "Hot Air Affair; a Modern Musical Par-
          able." Musical Opinion 91:489+, 6/68; Composer
          (Eng.) no.30:21-3, Winter 1968-69.
I92   Marcus, Leonard. "Game of the Name; Musical Per-
          sonages." High Fidelity and Musical America 23:4,
          1/73.
I93   Marek, George R. "Our Old Friend the Cigar Maker-
          ess; Program Notes." Opera News 32:6-7, 4/20/68.
I94   Marvill, George. "The Doh Boys (Modulator in the
          Classroom)." Music in Education 36:33 n.353, 1972.
I95   Matthews, Arthur C. " 'Matthews 37-1/2' (Aleatory
          Assembly of a Mixed-Media 'Son et Lumiere' Pastiche
          of an Exquisitely Meaningful Meaninglessness)."
          Stereo Review 29:74-6, 4/70.
       McElroy, George. SEE: Stedman, Jane W.
I96   McPherson, Jim. "Opera in Bright Lights: Familiar
          Works Retitled." Opera News 33:12-13, 4/5/69.
I97   Mendelsohn, John. "Superstardom Is My Destiny (Sa-
          tirical View of Pop-Rock Scene)." Rolling Stone n.
          82:24-7, 5/13/71.
I98   Minkler, Bill. "Performance Styles of Beginners."
          Music (A.G.O.) 7:42-3, 3/73.
I99   Moss, H. "Johann Sebastian Bach." Saturday Review
          55:66 n.45, 1972.
I100   Musical Opinion. "Organ at St. Freudeswide's, Toot-
          ing." Musical Opinion 94:307, 3/71.

I101 Musser, Willard I. "Female Oboists." Woodwind
      World 10:5 n.2, 1971.
I102 Nadel, Marc. "Thirty Years after (Rock Personalities)."
      Jazz and Pop 10:12-15, 4/71.
I103 Nathness, Sarah. "Tell It to the Marines." Opera
      News 35:20, 9/5/70.
I104 O'Keeffe, Vincent Charles. "Music and the Merrykins."
      Instrumentalist 24:51-2, 10/69.
I105 Opera Canada. "Rules for Visitors to the Court Opera,
      Vienna, 1897); extract from Wiener Sonn- und Mon-
      tagszeitung 8 Nov 1897. Opera Canada 12:14-15,
      n.1, 1971.
I106 Opera News. "Repress that Release!" Opera News 33:
      14-16, 2/1/69.
I107 _____. "The Second Caption (Pictures in Opera
      News's Files)." Opera News 32:13-15, 3/9/68.
I108 Pabiot, G. "Opinions sur Rue." Jazz Magazine n.184:
      25, 12/70.
I109 Padgett-Chandler, David E. "The Organ: an Agricul-
      tural Phenomenon." Musical Opinion 91:331+, 3/68.
I110 Page, Clifford. "Autolycus II." Musical Opinion 96:
      641, 9/73.
I111 Piano Quarterly. "The Beethoven-Schubert Complex Re-
      defined Together with Sundry Remarks Concerning
      Schubert's Unfinished Neuroses." Piano Quarterly
      8:24-8 n.69, 1969.
I112 Powell, Ross W. "A New Era for Wind Performers."
      Music Journal 26:52+, 4/68.
I113 Price, E. "Old Person's Guide to the 'Good King'."
      Music in Education 33:303, n.340, 1969.
I114 Reid, Robert L. "World's Greatest Composer." HiFi
      Stereo Review 21:102-4, 10/68.
I115 Reynolds, Gordon. "A Great Remarkable Fruit (Traits
      of an Examiner)." Music in Education 37:254-5,
      n.363, 1973.
I116 _____. "Minimum Requirements (a Humorous Look
      at the Music Profession)." Royal College of Music
      Magazine 67:101-3 n.3, 1971.
I117 _____. "Stale Cake." Music in Education 36:121-2
      n.355, 1972.
I118 Rich, Alan. "The 1984 Season--an Historic Document
      Is Brought to Light." Opera News 33:8-11, 1/4/69.
I119 Rich, Leslie. "How to Be a Music Critic; or, the Fine
      Art of Graceful Fakery." High Fidelity and Musical
      America 18:52-5, 5/68.
I120 Richardson, Viva Faye. "Music; Our 'Social' Inherit-
      ance." Music Journal 26:53, 1/68.

I121 _____. "Personal Tales of a Pianist." Music Jour-
        nal 28:48, 6/70.
I122 Rives, James A. "The Orchestral Musicians Compos-
        ing Committee." Instrumentalist 24:32+, 4/70.
I123 _____. "Revised Double Bass Curriculum." Instru-
        mentalist 25:20, 3/71.
I124 Roberts, Susan A. "Ringo and Violet: a Musical Ro-
        mance (between Two Afghan Hounds)." Music Jour-
        nal 27:36-7, 6/69.
I125 Rowland, Clarissa. "On First Setting Foot in the Albert
        Hall." Royal College of Music Magazine 67:60 n.2,
        1971.
I126 Rudoff, Harvey. "Historical Notes." Clavier 10:50
        n.1, 1971.
I127 _____. "Informal History of the Tuba." Music
        Journal 28:56, 5/70.
I128 _____. "Sale: Pianos and Pork Chops." Music
        Journal 29:76-7, 2/71.
I129 _____. "The Year in Computers (or, Input Paper
        and Output Cat)." Music Journal 28:38+, 7/70.
I130 _____. "You Were Expecting Maybe Ralph Nader?"
        Clavier 10:51 n.1, 1971.
I131 Ruzek, Donald H. "How to Play the Lagoon." Instru-
        mentalist 27:16, 12/72.
I132 _____. "My Visit to a Contrabassoon Factory."
        Instrumentalist 26:16, 1/72.
I133 Sack, Joe. "Musical Surprises." Arnold Bax Society
        Bulletin n.3:49-50, 10/68. Reprinted from Rand
        Daily Mail, 6/8/68.
I134 Saturday Review. "Table Talk in a Vienna Coffeehouse."
        Saturday Review 51:64, 5/11/68.
I135 Schoenstein, Ralph. "Twinkle, Twinkle, Little Star:
        Daddy Pushed You Where You Are." Today's Health
        51:26-8+, 6/73.
I136 Schwerke, Irving. "Composers as Human Beings;
        Reminiscences of a Life in Music." Stereo Review
        23:75-8, 11/69.
I137 Sheppard, Leslie. "Little Fiddle-Diddles." Strad 83:
        73+, 6/72.
I138 Sheresh, Beverly. "Grandfather's Blazing Trombone."
        Music Journal 27:50+, 9/69.
I139 Shultz, Henry. "Alkan; the Somewhat Imaginary Life
        and Times of the French Composer." Atlantic
        Monthly 232:80-3, 9/73; discussion, 232:49-50, 12/
        73 by Ralph Berkowitz.
I140 Simmonds, Ron. "Beef Stroganoff and Onion Spires."
        Crescendo International 11:12-13, 2/73.

I141 _____. "How High the C?" Crescendo International
          11:10-11, 3/73.
I142 Sorel, Claudette. "Musical Cat Tours Europe." Music
          Journal 28:24-5, 6/70.
I143 Starker, Janos. "Democracy in Music; a Fantasy Set
          in a Not-Too-Distant Future." High Fidelity and
          Musical America 23:62-4, 2/73.
I144 Stedman, Jane W. and McElroy, George. " 'Caro
          Nome': an Opera in Three Acts and Four Diction-
          aries." Opera News 32:6-7, 3/9/68.
I145 Stendahl. "Rossini Reminiscences"; reprinted from
          Stendahl's Life of Rossini. San Francisco Symphony
          Program Notes p. 10-11, 2/68.
I146 Stylites, S. "Organ Voluntary." Journal of Church
          Music 11:14-15, 9/69. Reprinted from the Christian
          Century, 10/29/58.
I147 Szantor, Jim. "The Trapezoid Papers." Down Beat
          39:12, 3/16/72.
I148 Toizer, Alfred. "It Sounds Like--a Concert-Goer's
          Guide to the Apt Adjective." HiFi Stereo Review
          20:44+, 3/68.
I149 Tomlinson, John W. "Mme. X." Opera News 34:16,
          1/31/70.
I150 Welch, C. "The Pop Computer (Identikit Pop Star)."
          Melody Maker 47:12, 8/12/72.
I151 West, John E. "St. Hilarious Undertone--an Account of
          an Outstanding Instrument." Musical Opinion 91:
          225+, 1/68.
I152 Wilson, George Y. "Some Random Notes on How to
          Make an April Fool's Speech." Your Musical Cue
          5:3-7 n.3, 1968-69.
I153 Wittering, T. T., pseud. "Edison Phonograph." Asso-
          ciation for Recorded Sound Collections Journal 4:65-
          9, n.1-3, 1972; reprinted from Studio Sound 4/72.
I154 Wood, Rupert M. "Concert Harmony." Strad 79:199+,
          9/68.
I155 YT-1708-A, Martian Culturescout, pseud. "Death of the
          Megaband." Instrumentalist 27:70-2, 10/72.
I156 Zeschin, Robert. "Food and Lodging; an Irreverent
          Traveler's Guide to Operaland." Opera News 36:6-
          7, 4/1/72.
I157 _____. "The Savoyard 'Ring,' or, a Tetralogy."
          Opera News 35:6-7, 4/3/71.

PLACES AND TRAVEL

J1   Ace, Goodman. "Hospital Hospitality: Mount Sinai
      Hospital." Saturday Review 55:6, 5/6/72.
J2   Andersen, Jane Lee. "Expectant Pleasures." Travel
      129:63-4, 3/68.
J3   Atcheson, Richard. "Encounter in London." Holiday
      46:10-11, 8/69.
J4   Barthelme, Donald. "Paraguay." New Yorker 45:32-4,
      9/6/69.
J5   Bernstein, Leonard S. "How to Stop Them after
      They've Photographed Paris; Sabotaging an Evening
      of Slide Viewing." House Beautiful 114:171-2, 10/72.
J6   Bozell, L. Brent, Jr. "Sixteen Year Old's European
      Vacation." National Review 25:895+, 8/17/73.
J7   Brennan, John. "Gould Theory." National Review 21:
      802, 8/12/69.
J8   Buchwald, Art. "Airline Rate War." Holiday 47:88,
      2/70.
J9   Buckley, William Frank, Jr. "Getting About in Italy;
      Baggage Porters." National Review 25:1075, 9/28
      /73.
J10   Burgess, Anthony, pseud. "Letter from Europe."
      American Scholar 40:514+; 41:139-42, Summer,
      Winter 1971; 425-8, Summer 1972; 42:135-8, Winter
      1972.
J11   Caples, John. "Madison Avenue." Saturday Review
      52:57-8, 2/8/69.
J12   Carson, L. M. Kit. "Opinion: On the Magick Coun-
      try." Mademoiselle 67:24+, 7/68.
J13   Ciardi, John. "Duel of Honor." Saturday Review 52:
      14-15, 3/15/69.
J14   _____. Manner of Speaking: "Change of Name for
      Grant's Tomb." Saturday Review 51:90, 3/9/68.
J15   Commonweal. "Moon Game." Commonweal 90:476-7,
      8/8/69.
J16   DeKay, Ormonde, Jr. "Continental Drip." Horizon

15:118-19, Winter 1973.

J17   Ephron, Nora. "Beach Wife." Holiday 45:68-9+, 5/69.

J18   Everett, Barbara. "Greened-In Again." Saturday Review 55:16, 2/12/72.

J19   Flythe, Starkey, Jr. "From Atlanta to the Sea." Holiday 51:4+ 3/72.

J20   Fortune. "Dining Aloft: A Dyspeptic View." Fortune 77:120-1, 3/68.

J21   Francois, Andre. "Fun with John and Mary and Jet Lag"; Drawings. Holiday 43:64-9, 3/68.

J22   Frayn, Michael. "This Earth, This Realm, This Plastic Finnan Haddie." Horizon 11:120, Summer 1969.

J23   Gannon, Thomas M. "Urbanology." America 122:8-10, 1/10/70.

J24   Gittelson, Natalie. "Train Yourself to Relax." Harper's Bazaar 101:11+, 8/68.

J25   Greenfield, Meg. "Gossip Gap." Newsweek 84:37, 9/16/74.

J26   Hodes, Arthur W. "Sentimental Journey: New York Revisited." Down Beat 36:36, 11/13/69.

J27   Jay, Alexander. "Another Farewell to New York." National Review 24:1010, 9/15/72.

J28   Johnston, William. "Up Up and Awry!" Holiday 54: 26-8+, 7/73.

J29   Kanfer, Stefan. "Candid in New York." New York Times Magazine p. 60+, 9/24/72.

J30   Keefauver, John. "It's Fun! To Europe for $19.99." National Review 25:466, 4/27/73.

J31   Kerr, Jean. "I Want to Go Down to the Sea Again." Holiday 47:16-18, 6/70.

J32   Knott, James Proctor. "Untold Delights of Duluth"; Address, January 27, 1871, ed. by D. G. McCullough. American Heritage 22:76-80, 6/71.

J33   Kozlick, Joseph C. "Life in a Spanish Boatyard." Motor Boating 123:60-1+, 2/69.

J34   Kubik, Gail T. "An American (Composer) in Paris and Elsewhere." Music Educators Journal 55:40-5, 5/69.

J35   Lipez, Richard. "Back on the Track." Progressive 38:22, 2/74.

J36   Lowe, David. "Kentucky on $5 a Day." Esquire 71: 88+, 3/69.

J37   Martin, Edward Winslow, pseud. "Fun City One Hundred Years Ago"; excerpts from The Secrets of the Great City, comp. by G. M. Naimark. Holiday 47: 82+, 2/70.

J38   McCall, Bruce. "Discovery of the East Pole." Harper's 249:8-9, 11/74.

J39   McElwaine, Sandra. "Great Washington Quiz Game."
          Vogue 162:69, 7/73.
J40   Meehan, Thomas. "Rob and Barbi Go Brownstoning."
          New York Times Magazine p.32-3+, 11/22/70; re-
          ply, P. Wilkes and J. Wilkes, p.144, 12/6/70.
J41   Merrill, Grayson. "Chesapeake Revisited." Motor
          Boating 121:44-7+, 4/68.
J42   Nadel, Michael. "If This Be Profane: Establishing a
          Craters-of-the-Moon-on-the-Moon National Monument."
          Living Wilderness 33:2, Summer 1969.
J43   New York Magazine. "Classic New York Jokebook."
          New York Magazine 6:24+, 8/27/73.
J44   New Yorker. "Fire." New Yorker 48:32-3, 3/4/72.
J45   _____. "Undivided Attention." New Yorker 47:20-
          3, 7/10/71.
J46   Newman, Edwin. "Steak Media, Please." Atlantic
          Monthly 230:98-100, 9/72.
J47   O'Higgins, Patrick. "Two Dames at Sea." McCall's
          97:38+, 2/70.
J48   Perelman, Sidney Joseph. "I Dreamt that I Dwelt in
          Marble Halls." Holiday 44:56-7+, 9/68.
J49   _____. "Room and Bored; Why Not Rent an Irish
          Castle for a Week or Two?" Holiday 45:40-1+,
          3/69.
J50   Peterson, O. "Tales of Manhattan." Jazz Monthly
          n.175:9-10, 9/69.
J51   Porges, Paul Peter. "Father Knows Best; Trip to
          Europe." Holiday 51:32-7, 1/72.
J52   Raphael, Chalm. "Plane Flight." Atlantic Monthly
          221:122, 2/68.
J53   Reader's Digest. "Summer's Idyll." Reader's Digest
          94:110-12, 6/69.
J54   Rhoades, Jonathan. "Going from Bad to Wurst; Euro-
          pean Drivers." Sports Illustrated 37:78-82+, 8/28/
          72.
J55   Richardson, Jack. "Witch of Las Vegas." Esquire
          77:104-7+, 1/72.
J56   Rosten, Leo. "London Notebook." Look 32:10, 5/14/
          68.
J57   _____. "Odd Memories; Travel Recollections."
          Saturday Review World 1:22-3, 11/20/73.
J58   Schoenstein, Ralph. "Don't Let Anyone Catch You Using
          Your Naked Eye." Today's Health 49:28-31, 6/71.
J59   Smith, Elinor Goulding. "What! You're Not Going to
          Thorshavn?" Travel 136:74-6, 12/71.
J60   Solomon, Barbara Probst. "Back to Madrid"; excerpts.
          Harper's 239:76-89, 8/69.

J61   Sorauer, Helly. "How I Conquered the Australian
       Alps." Travel and Camera 32:31-2, 5/69.
J62   Steinfels, Peter. "Surviving in New York." Common-
       weal 93:513, 2/26/71.
J63   Strout, Cushing. "Man in the Ruins: From a Roman
       Journal." Yale Review 61:151-60, 10/71.
J64   Viorst, Judith. "Two Weeks in Another Town." Red-
       book 137:62-3+, 8/71.
J65   Walton, Mary Dumas. "Half the Fun of a Trip...."
       Harvest Years 8:46-7, 8/68.
J66   Waugh, Alec. "Lost Trains." National Review 20:
       870, 8/27/68.

POLITICS AND GOVERNMENT

K1 Ace, Goodman. "Cut-Rate President." Saturday Review 55:4, 1/1/72.

K2 _____. "If You Were President." Saturday Review 54:8, 1/30/71.

K3 _____. "Oh, Say Can't You See?" Saturday Review 53:8, 12/5/70.

K4 _____. "Peace Unearthed." Saturday Review World 2:32, 9/21/74.

K5 _____. "Scion." Saturday Review 54:6, 10/30/71.

K6 _____. "What in the World!" Saturday Review 54:4, 7/3/71.

K7 Allen, Steve and Trumbo, Dalton. "Happy Jack Fish Hatchery Papers"; letters. Esquire 73:73-7+, 1/70.

K8 Allen, Woody. "Schmeed Memoirs." New Yorker 47:36-7, 4/17/71.

K9 Angell, Roger. "Floto Letters: Dear Mayor Floto." New Yorker 46:34-7, 2/21/70.

K10 _____. "Pierre Rumblings." New Yorker 44:58-9, 12/14/68.

K11 _____. "Please Hang Up, I'm Expecting a Nuisance Call." New Yorker 47:30-1, 2/12/72.

K12 Angst, Ernst. "Liberal's Lexicon"; excerpts from So You Want to Be a Liberal? National Review 21:1177, 11/18/69.

K13 Armed Forces Journal. "From Stem to Stern--the Tightest Ship Afloat." Armed Forces Journal 110:32-6, 10/72.

K14 _____. "Once a Marine, Always a Marine." Armed Forces Journal 10:34-5+, 11/72.

K15 _____. " 'Valley Forge, Custer's Ranks, San Juan Hill and Patton's Tanks...' An Army Is Born." Armed Forces Journal 109:34-5+, 6/72.

K16 Aurand, Evan P. "Tiger Hunting in Dinglabash." United States Naval Institute Proceedings 100:35-9, 6/74.

K17 Aurthur, Robert Alan. "Hanging Out." Esquire 76:
     46+, 11/72.

K18 Baker, Russell. "Conservative Chic." New York
     Times Magazine p. 6, 10/21/73.

K19 _____. "Conversation Piece." New York Times
     Magazine p. 6, 3/2/74.

K20 _____. "Cultivated Killing." New York Times Mag-
     azine p. 6, 10/7/73.

K21 _____. "Hollywood-on-the-Potomac." New York
     Times Magazine p. 6, 2/10/74.

K22 _____. "Honker at the Pentagon." New York Times
     Magazine p. 6, 5/6/73.

K23 _____. "House Is a Home." New York Times Mag-
     azine p. 6, 11/4/73.

K24 _____. "Picking of the President, 1968"; with edi-
     torial comment. Saturday Evening Post 241:19-23+,
     70, 3/9/68.

K25 _____. "Seeing America." New York Times Maga-
     zine p. 6, 6/17/73.

K26 _____. "A Shiny New Haldeman, and a ... Letter
     to Santa Claus." New York Times Magazine p. 6,
     12/16/73.

K27 _____. "Turkey Tapes." New York Times Maga-
     zine p. 6, 11/18/73.

K28 _____. "Vintage Farce." New York Times Maga-
     zine p. 4, 12/30/73.

K29 _____. "Who Is the Man in the White House?"
     Look 33:92+, 12/16/69.

K30 _____. "Work Fanatics; Work Habits of White House
     Staff Members." New York Times Magazine p. 4,
     8/19/73.

K31 Barrett, George H. "Amplify and Exaggerate." USAF
     Instructors Journal 8:18-20, Winter 1970-71.

K32 Bassett, Warren L. "Cryptic Bulletin from American
     Interior." Harper's 247:86, 7/73.

K33 Benchley, Robert Charles. "Paul Revere's Ride"; ex-
     cerpt from The Early Worm. Saturday Evening Post
     244:58-9, Winter 1972.

K34 Brickman, Marshall. "Recipes of Chairman Mao."
     New Yorker 49:24-5, 8/27/73.

K35 Brooks, Paul. "When Kids Write their Congressman."
     America 122:341-2, 3/28/70.

K36 Bryant, Traphes L. "My Life in the White House Dog-
     house"; excerpt from An Outrageous White House Di-
     ary, ed. by Frances Spatz Leighton. Ladies' Home
     Journal 89:108-9+, 11/72.

K37 Buchwald, Art. "Of Beds and Body Counts: Interpre-

tation of Art Buchwald." Newsweek 71:82+, 2/19/
68.

K38 _____. "Pre-Election Fun: a Chat with George
Washington." Seventeen 31:166+, 10/72.

K39 Buckley, William Frank, Jr. "Notes and Asides."
National Review 22:20, 1/13/70.

K40 Canfield, Roger B. "Uncommon Cause: the Snails in
Miami." National Review 24:100, 2/4/72.

K41 Capp, Al. "Henry and the Pres." Saturday Evening
Post 244:42-7+, Winter 1972.

K42 Cary, Eve. "Love on the Left." Mademoiselle 67:75+,
10/68.

K43 Catledge, Turner. "Our Town's Only Republican"; excerpt from My Life and the Times. Reader's Digest
101:133-5, 8/72.

K44 Chamberlin, Anne. "How I Learned to Stop Worrying
and Trust the State Department." Saturday Evening
Post 241:34-7, 7/13/68.

K45 Christian Century. "Grapes of Wrath: V. C. Communi-
que." Christian Century 86:1005, 7/23/69.

K46 _____. "Making of a President, 1968." Christian
Century 85:1387, 10/30/68.

K47 _____. "Please, Mr. Ho!" Christian Century 85:
127, 1/24/68.

K48 _____. "War Games." Christian Century 86:913,
7/2/69.

K49 Ciardi, John. "Manner of Speaking." Saturday Review
World 1:12, 9/11/73.

K50 _____. "Tour of Duty." Saturday Review 53:4+,
12/19/70.

K51 Collier, Barnard Law. "Mastermind as Mouthpiece."
Saturday Review 55:8-9, 11/18/72.

K52 Commonweal. "Report from the Future." Commonweal 91:239, 11/21/69.

K53 Coyne, John R., Jr. "Peace in Our Time: On Campus and Off." National Review 21:285+, 3/25/69.

K54 Davidson, Carla. "Good Lord, Grandpa, It All Came
True." American Heritage 22:70-1, 2/71.

K55 DeCamp, Dot. "Smith/Jones." Library Journal 95:
3451, 10/15/70.

K56 Dunne, Finley Peter. "Mr. Dooley on The Hague Conference, 1907." American Heritage 22:6, 2/71.

K57 Eastlake, William. "Whitey's on the Moon Now."
Nation 209:238-9, 9/15/69.

Eliscu, Edward. SEE: Sorel, Edward.

K58 Ellis, H. F. "Content of Tables: Conference Tables,
1969-2169." New Yorker 45:102+, 2/22/69.

K59   Elson, Peter M. "Humor Is No Laughing Matter!"
       Infantry 62:16-19, 3-4/72.
K60   Esquire. "Welcome to the Nixon Style." Esquire 71:
       87-91, 6/69.
K61   _____. "White House Garage Sale." Esquire 80:
       62-3, 8/73.
K62   Events, Rolling and Nofact, Robert, pseuds. "Inside
       Report: Takeover Plot by the Extremeblackpower-
       newleft." Ramparts 7:16, 9/7/68.
K63   Everett, Barbara. "Insectual Politics." Saturday Re-
       view 54:68, 11/20/71.
K64   Eyre, Charles F. "Re: How Segregation Ended in the
       Early Seventies." National Review 23:1303-4,
       11/19/71.
K65   Faber, Harold. "What Was Ulysses S. Grant's First
       Name? Presidential Trivia." New York Times
       Magazine p. 69+, 9/10/72.
K66   Fagan, Dennis. "All in the Fallacy." National Review
       26:703, 6/21/74.
K67   Fernandez, Miller. "Crib Sheets for the President."
       Atlas 21:36-7, 1/72.
K68   Fulsom, Don. "Tricky Quiz; Fifty Trivial Questions
       about the President." Esquire 77:124-5, 3/72.
K69   Gardner, Martin. "Doctor Matrix Gives His Explana-
       tion of Why Mr. Nixon Was Elected President."
       Scientific American 220:116-18+, 1/69.
K70   Gold, Victor. "Commission on Commissions." Na-
       tional Review 22:1038, 10/6/70.
K71   _____. "On Disengagement: Limit of Former John-
       son Administration Officials to their Involvement in
       U.S. Government Affairs." National Review 21:790,
       8/12/69.
K72   Gray, Paul Edward. "My Three Weeks at the White
       House." New Yorker 45:32-3, 5/17/69.
K73   Halloran, Barney. "Ghosts on Your Post?" Soldiers,
       Official U.S. Army Magazine 27:30-6, 10/72.
K74   Harkins, William E. "A. K. Tolstoi's Parody 'History
       of the Russian State'." Slavic Review 27:459-69,
       9/68.
K75   Harrissy, Louis J. "Nation Is Moving to the Left."
       National Review 22:260, 3/10/70.
K76   Hochman, Sandra. "China Fantasy." Harper's Bazaar
       105:62, 1/72.
K77   Hope, Francis. "Knowing the Form." New Statesman
       83:789-90, 6/9/72.
K78   Jay, Alexander. "Lindsay Papers." National Review
       23:990, 9/10/71.

K79   Jeffries, Jean. "Chetsky-Davidov Report." National
       Review 21:748, 7/29/69.
K80   Jensen, Oliver. "They're Keeping It Hushed Up."
       Harper's 249:48, 12/74.
K81   Keefauver, John. "How Henry J. Littlefinger Licked
       the Hippies' Scheme to Take Over the Country by
       Tossing Pot in Postage Stamp Glue." National Re-
       view 23:1180+, 10/22/71.
K82   _____. "Save the Trailer Parks!" National Review
       26:592, 5/24/74.
K83   Keillor, Garrison. "Congress in Crisis; the Proximity
       Bill." New Yorker 49:36-7, 4/7/73.
K84   _____. "United States Still on Top, Says Rest of
       World." New Yorker 47:35, 10/2/71.
K85   Kitman, Marvin. "Make Me an Offer." Newsweek 84:
       23, 11/11/74.
K86   Life. Partin Shots: "A Cabinet for All Reasons."
       Life 70:67-8, 1/29/71.
K87   _____. Parting Shots: "Proposing Some Memorable
       Commemoratives." Life 70:66A-68, 2/26/71.
K88   Lipez, Richard. "Great Enunciator." Newsweek 83:
       15, 3/18/74.
K89   _____. "New Morality." Progressive 38:66, 9/74.
K90   Look. "Look Invites You to Play the City Game."
       Look 32:104-5, 6/11/68.
K91   Matthews, Jeff. "Trial of Ivan Dissentovich." Nation-
       al Review 25:1158, 10/26/73.
K92   McClaughry, John. "Looking Backward: 1976."
       Harvard Review 4 no. 2:39-48, 1968.
K93   McNeil, Lily. "Dream." New Yorker 49:25, 9/3/73.
K94   McWhirter, William A. "When (and If) Better Presi-
       dents Are Made." Harper's Bazaar 102:148-9+,
       1/69.
K95   Meehan, Thomas. "Abraham Lincoln: Lawyer, States-
       man, and Golf Nut." New Yorker 47:35-6, 8/28/71.
K96   _____. "Scram Gets Green Light; Spiro Agnew to
       Rise at Marshgrass." New Yorker 44:32-3, 2/15/
       69.
K97   Metzger, Louis. "It All Counts on Thirty: The
       Diver." Marine Corps Gazette 54:43-4, 1/70.
K98   Mounier, Andre. "Reciprocity; with Reprint of News
       Column." National Review 20:388-9, 4/23/68.
K99   Mount, Ferdinand. "Viewed from London." National
       Review 20:1217, 12/3/68.
K100   National Review. "Give This Man a Blank Check?"
       National Review 20:276+, 3/26/68.
K101   _____. "Here It Comes...." National Review 23:

24, 1/12/71.

K102 _____. "Julius Caesar Crosses the Rubicon." National Review 20:328, 4/9/68.

K103 _____. "Secret Strategy of Nelson Aldrich Rockefeller, the Shrewdly Conceived Grand Battle Plan of
Richard Milhous Nixon, and the Diabolically Ostensible Recalcitrance of Ronald B. Reagan." National
Review 20:327+, 4/9/68.

K104 _____. "Thoughts of Chairman Mao, no. 82: Hero-
ic Air Squadron." National Review 20:389, 4/23/68.

K105 New Republic. TRB from Washington: "Firstest with
the Mostest." New Republic 166:2, 3/25/72.

K106 _____. TRB from Washington: "Imaginary Conversation with the Washington Monument Executive Man-
sion and Memorial." New Republic 163:4, 7/4/70.

K107 _____. TRB from Washington: "Swift Solution:
Use of Small, Tactical Nuclear Weapons in Laos."
New Republic 164:4, 3/20/71.

K108 New Yorker. Notes and Comment: "Imaginary Hear-
ing on the Success or Failure of the War on the
Basis of Effort Rather than Results." New Yorker
46:47-8, 12/5/70.

K109 _____. Notes and Comment: "An Imaginary Speech
on the Problems of the Nation." New Yorker 46:
31-2, 12/19/70.

K110 Newsweek. "Double Take; Altered Nixon Speech."
Newsweek 83:19, 1/14/74.

K111 _____. "Of Beds and Body Counts; Interpretation of
Art Buchwald." Newsweek 71:82+, 2/19/68.

K112 Novick, Sheldon. Jaundiced Eye: "Project Independ-
ence." Environment 16:inside cover, 11/74.

K113 Orth, Maureen. "Fryeing the President." Newsweek
82:71, 1/28/74.

K114 Plumb, J. H. "Political Pornography." Horizon 14:
18-9, Winter 1972.

K115 Resting, James. "In My Nation." Ramparts 7:15,
9/7/68.

K116 Rickenbacker, William F. "Interview (Nixon)." National Review 24:224, 3/3/72.

K117 _____. "Willmoore Wheeler Rides Again." National Review 23:1181, 10/22/71.

K118 Robb, Lynda Bird (Johnson). "Memo to Campaigners."
McCall's 95:32+, 8/68.

K119 Rothschild, Emma. "Infiltrating Nixon." Ramparts
7:38-9, 12/14/68.

Sale, Kirkpatrick. SEE: Sorel, Edward.

K120 Schoenstein, Ralph. "Plowshares, Anyone?" New

Yorker 47:52-3, 12/11/71.

K121 Schweitz, Bob. "How Omar Bradley Got to Be a Major." Air Force Times (Eastern edition) 34:13, 7/24/74.

K122 Segal, Erich Wolf. "Night They Auctioned Off the Roman Empire." Horizon 13:36-9, Summer 1971.

K123 Senior Scholastic. "Campaign Trail: Snoopy-for-President Campaign: Why It Can't Succeed." Senior Scholastic 93:2-5, 10/11/68.

K124 _____. "Iron Mountain Controversy: Painful Economics or Political Hoax?" Senior Scholastic 92: 10-12, 4/4/68.

K125 Sievers, Harry J. "Noble Knights of the Gridiron." America 118:367, 3/23/68.

K126 Silverman, Paul. "Party Line." Saturday Review 53: 10, 9/12/70.

K127 Sisyphus, pseud. "Notes on the Bicentennial." Commonweal 100:396-7, 7/26/74.

K128 Sorel, Edward. "Richard M. Nixon Library; Some Modest Proposals." Atlantic Monthly 227:85-92, 2/71.

K129 _____ and Eliscu, Edward. "Handbook for the Virgin Voter." Ramparts 12:42-4, 11/73.

K130 _____ and Sale, Kirkpatrick. "Modest Proposal: on Increasing Respect for the President." Ramparts 11:30-3, 4/73.

K131 Starnes, Richard. "Buster Big-Brain's Revenge." Field & Stream 74:22+, 10/69.

K132 Steinfels, Peter. "Changing Your Spots." Commonweal 93:166, 11/13/70.

K133 _____. "Day They Stole the Agnew." Commonweal 93:390+, 1/22/71.

K134 _____. "Mr. Dooley in Peace and War." Commonweal 92:262, 5/29/70.

K135 Stevenson, James. "Metropolitan Comics"; comic strip. New Yorker 47:36-9, 7/17/71.

K136 Terrill, Ross. "Inscrutable West." Atlantic Monthly 226:68-71, 8/70.

K137 Thompson, Stephen. "Arsenal of Appeasement." National Review 22:769, 7/28/70.

K138 Time. "What Else?" Time 91:15-16, 6/28/68.

K139 _____. "What Nixon Might Have Said; Rewriting his Phoenix Speech." Time 96:28, 11/16/70.

K140 Today's Education. "Suggested Menu to Nourish the Body Politic." Today's Education 58:42-3, 2/69.

K141 Tran-van-Dinh. "Another Open Letter to President Nixon." Christian Century 86:1137-8, 9/3/69.

K142 Trans-Action. "Comment: Social Science Fiction:
      Report from Iron Mountain"; symposium. Trans-
      Action 5:6-20, 1/68. Reply, L. C. Lewin, 5:2+,
      4/68.
K143 Trillin, Calvin. "I Met Khrushchev and Didn't Argue
      about Refrigerators." Atlantic Monthly 229:88-90,
      3/72.
K144 _____. "Profiles in Courrèges." Atlantic Monthly
      228:121-3, 11/71.
     Trumbo, Dalton. SEE: Allen, Steve.
K145 Vogue. "November 7, 1972 and Where Are You?"
      Vogue 160:164-5, 11/1/72.
K146 Von Dreele, W. H. "Hubert Humphrey Sings Old-Time
      Favorites." National Review 20:995, 10/8/68.
K147 Watson, Craig M. "Arcania; a Fable." Newsweek 83:
      11, 2/25/74.
K148 Wheeler, Timothy J., pseud. "Dime's Worth of Dif-
      ference Candidate Profile Analysis Theorem." Na-
      tional Review 20:1116, 11/5/68.
K149 _____. "Our People's Underworld Movement Ex-
      posed." National Review 21:376-81, 4/22/69.
K150 Yoakum, Robert. "Everybody's Got a Message." New
      Republic 159:17, 11/2/68.
K151 Zinsser, William Knowlton. "My Table Can Lick Your
      Table." Life 66:14, 1/24/69.
K152 _____. "New China Policy in Rock Glade, New Jer-
      sey." New York Times Magazine p. 35-6, 2/6/72.
K153 _____. "Upward Failure; Case Study of a Strange
      American Phenomenon." Life 73:45-6+, 3/31/72.
K154 _____. "What Happened when Refractory and Brake
      Ran Afoul of the U.S. Godwit Lobby; a Fantasy."
      Life 68:42-3, 4/24/70.

RELIGION, PHILOSOPHY, AND OCCULT SCIENCES

L1 Allen, Woody. "Examining Psychic Phenomena." New
  Yorker 48:32-3, 10/7/72.

L2 _____. "Fabulous Tales and Mythical Beasts."
  New Republic 171:19-21, 11/30/74.

L3 _____. "Hassidic Tales with a Guide to their Interpretation by the Noted Scholar." New Yorker 46:
  31-2, 6/20/70.

L4 _____. "My Philosophy." New Yorker 45:25-6,
  12/27/69.

L5 Angell, Roger. "Your Horoscope." New Yorker 45:
  33, 3/29/69.

L6 Baker, Russell. "Sexorcist." New York Times Magazine p. 6, 2/17/74.

L7 Barker, H. T. "Under the Spreading Grapefruit Tree."
  Reader's Digest 103:198-200, 11/73.

L8 Barrett, J. Edward. "Preliminary Report of the Presidential Commission on the Christian Conspiracy."
  Christian Century 85:166-7, 2/7/68.

L9 Barthelme, Donald. "Teachings of Don B: a Yankee
  Way of Knowledge." New York Times Magazine p.
  14-15+, 2/11/73.

L10 Bledsoe, Jerry C. "Brother's Keeper." Esquire 76:
  76:81-2+, 11/71.

L11 Blood, Chris, pseud. "War Games." Christian Century 85:411-13, 4/3/68.

L12 Bolton, Thomas. "Night My Stars Got Crossed."
  Reader's Digest 99:123-5, 12/71.

L13 Brennan, John. "Where Are You, Fr. O'Brien?
  Where Are You, Fr. Fitzgerald?" National Review
  21:231+, 3/11/69.

L14 Byrne, Robert. "Bless Me, Father"; excerpt from
  Memories of a Non-Jewish Boyhood. Commonweal
  93:519+, 2/26/71.

L15 Christian Century. "Adventures of Superhawk." Christian Century 86:391, 3/19/68.

L16 _____. "Beautiful Lethargy." Christian Century
88:915, 7/28/71.

L17 _____. "Churchgoing, Washington Style; Services at
the White House." Christian Century 86:271, 2/19/
69.

L18 _____. "Creatio ex Nihilo." Christian Century 86:
1437, 11/5/69.

L19 _____. "Death, Be Proud." Christian Century 85:
635, 5/8/68.

L20 _____. "Ecumenical Emergencies." Christian Century 85:1067, 8/21/68.

L21 _____. "Fine Theological Points." Christian Century 86:31, 1/1/69.

L22 _____. "Instant Tradition: Think Ethnic!" Christian Century 85:1187, 9/18/68.

L23 _____. "Killed with the Holy Ghost." Christian
Century 88:939, 8/4/71.

L24 _____. "Ministerial Images." Christian Century 86:
1125, 8/27/69.

L25 _____. "Out from Under; Underground Church
Kicked Upstairs." Christian Century 86:239, 2/12/69

L26 _____. Pen-Ultimate: "Ministerial Maneuvers."
Christian Century 85:1091, 8/28/68.

L27 _____. Pen-Ultimate: "Sunday School Come-Ons."
Christian Century 85:1027, 8/14/68.

L28 _____. Pen-Ultimate: "Wit and Witlessness."
Christian Century 85:979, 7/31/68.

L29 _____. "Prayerful Sonorities for Senatorial Snor-
ers." Christian Century 86:965, 7/16/69.

L30 _____. "Project Fork Over." Christian Century 86:
825, 6/11/69.

L31 _____. "Protocol for Campus Pastors." Christian
Century 86:1297, 10/8/69.

L32 _____. "Religious Series Plans Soul Transplants."
Christian Century 85:349, 3/20/68.

L33 _____. "Revivalism Revisited." Christian Century
86:135, 1/22/69.

L34 _____. "Scenario for the Movement: the Jesus
Revolution." Christian Century 88:843, 7/7/71.

L35 _____. "Seek Ye First..." Christian Century 87:
519, 4/22/70.

L36 _____. "Silent Majority Sings." Christian Century
86:1533, 11/26/69.

L37 _____. "Veneration Gap." Christian Century 86:
761, 5/28/69.

L38 Coffin, T. Eugene. "Genesis 1969." Christianity Today 13:7, 1/17/69.

L39 Cunneen, Sally. "Misunderstood Motives of Jacqueline
        Onassis." Christian Century 86:15, 1/1/69.
L40 Eisenberg, Lee and Ferrell, Tom. "Five Sleazy
        Pieces." Esquire 78:140-1, 8/72.
L41 Elkoff, Marvin. "Some of My Kid's Best Friends Are
        Black." Esquire 76:10+, 12/71.
L42 Esquire. "Puke Ethics." Esquire 72:100-1, 9/69.
     Ferrell, Tom. SEE: Eisenberg, Lee.
L43 Gardner, Martin. "Dr. Matrix Brings his Numerologi-
        cal Science to Bear on the Occult Powers of the
        Pyramid." Scientific American 230:116-21, 6/74.
L44 Hiltner, Seward. "Good Old Summertime? Pastoral
        Aestivation." Christian Century 91:771-3, 8/7/74.
L45 Holiday. "Darn Clever, These Chinese." Holiday 50:
        41, 11/71.
L46 Holland, Barbara. "Horoscopes for Other People."
        McCall's 100:56+, 6/73.
L47 Keefauver, John. "Of the Black Whites and the White
        Blacks." National Review 24:901, 8/18/72.
L48 King, Larry L. "Confessions of a White Racist."
        Harper's 240:63-6+, 1/70.
L49 Levenson, Sam. "Men in Mama's Life." Ladies'
        Home Journal 87:24+, 5/70; Reader's Digest 97:41-
        4, 9/70.
L50 Life. Parting Shots: "Prejudice among the Penguins."
        Life 68:77-80, 5/1/70.
L51 MacMullen, Howard H., Jr. "Times Report Boosts
        Future of Hope." Christian Century 85:818-19,
        6/19/68.
L52 Marty, Martin E. "Well Timed Piety." Christian
        Century 89:995, 10/4/72.
L53 Mehle, Aileen. "You Can Always Tell a Gemini."
        Harper's Bazaar 101:216-17, 10/68.
L54 Miller, Floyd. "Yoga and Me." Reader's Digest 100:
        101-4, 3/72.
L55 Parenteau, Shirley. "Better Boating with the Stars."
        Motor Boating 127:82-3, 1/71.
L56 Ramsay, J. and Ramsay, K. "How to Succeed on a
        Committee without Really Thinking." Christianity
        Today 13:8-9, 1/3/69.
L57 Schoenstein, Ralph. "Psychics at the Scrimmage Line."
        Today's Health 52:48-51, 10/74.
L58 Schutjer, Clifford D. "Five Editorials." Christian
        Century 86:449-50, 4/2/69.
L59 Stees, Arthur R. "Demittals, Unlimited." Christian
        Century 90:176-8+, 2/7/73.
L60 Steinfels, Peter. "Anyone for Ecological Theology?"

Commonweal 91:576, 2/27/70.

L61 _____. "I Was a Catholic for the PAX." Commonweal 92:454, 9/18/70.

L62 Stevens, Edward. "Dateline: Jupiter 2500 Report from
Committee Hearings on Interplanetary Morality."
New Catholic World 215:196-7+, 9/72.

L63 Stine, Bob. "Afternoon with an Astrologer: a Predictable Visit." Senior Scholastic 97:42, 10/26/70.

L64 Tomkins, Calvin. "Teachings of Joe Pye; Field Notes
for Carlos Castaneda's Next Epiphany." New Yorker
48:37-8, 2/3/73.

L65 Tresilian, Liz. "Dog Horoscopes"; excerpts from The
Dog Horoscope Book. Saturday Evening Post 243:
118-9, Fall 1971; 244:36, Spring 1972.

L66 Trillin, Calvin. "Lester Drentluss Turns Black with
Desire." Atlantic Monthly 222:71-3, 11/68.

L67 Tullius, F. P. "Mantras for Everyone." New Yorker
50:43, 12/2/74.

L68 _____. "Unpsychic Man of the Year." New Yorker
50:29, 6/24/74.

L69 Woodrum, Lon. "After Death the Judgment." Christianity Today 12:16, 7/19/68.

L70 _____. "Convert." Christianity Today 14:17, 6/5/
70.

L71 _____. "Dark Counsel at Easter." Christianity Today 14:10, 3/27/70.

L72 _____. "If Dropouts Turn On." Christianity Today
14:18-19, 10/24/69.

SCIENCE, ENGINEERING, MATHEMATICS AND TECHNOLOGY

M1   Abrahams, Paul. "Compiler Pessimization." Datama-
      tion 17:32-3, 4/1/71.
M2   American City. "Funny Thing Happened on the Way to
      the Incinerator." American City 83:6, 5/68.
M3   Amos, Wayne. "Quiet Sounds around Us." Good
      Housekeeping 166:83+, 5/68.
M4   Armour, Richard. "Why I'm Not a Bird Watcher."
      Saturday Review 54:58, 10/30/71.
M5   Baker, Russell. "Great Whale's Mistake." New York
      Times Magazine p. 6, 6/23/74.
M6   _____. "Poodlepower." New York Times Magazine
      p. 6, 6/3/73.
M7   _____. "Wise Words on Weeds." Reader's Digest
      103:143-4, 8/73.
M8   Benchley, Peter. "Prognosticators." New Yorker 48:
      50-1, 11/25/72.
M9   Berenson, Ruth. "Nature vs. Nurture." National Re-
      view 26:821+, 7/19/74.
M10   Berenyi, Ivan. "British Have a Thing about Com-
      puters." Office 77:35+, 3/73.
M11   Betzelberger, H. R. "How I Trained My Wife to Buy
      Repairs." Farm Journal 95:39, 6/71.
M12   Bissey, Jack E. "Friday Experiments." Journal of
      Chemical Education 46:497-8, 8/69.
M13   Bland, Frederick. "Scenario for the Interactive 70's."
      Datamation 15:101+, 10/69.
M14   Blodax, Eric. "Also Sprach von Neumann." Datama-
      tion 16:104+, 1/70; 74-7, 3/70; 93-6, 5/70; 118-21,
      6/70; 17:44-6+, 5/15/71; 18:60-1+, 3/72; 82-5+,
      10/72.
      Bodine, Lloyd T. SEE: Yates, Brock.
M15   Brachman, Michael. "Ion, My Love." Chemistry 45:
      32, 10/72.

M16 Bracken, Peg. "Not with a Bang but a Hiccup." Sat-
     urday Review 53:3, 12/26/70.
M17 Braun, Dick. "Final Solution to Pollution." Farm
     Journal 96:D16, 4/72.
M18 Brien, Alan. "Sun, the Sun!" New Statesman 76:12,
     7/5/68.
M19 Brix, Christian L. "Twentieth Century Fable: the
     Saga of Old Charlie." Infosystems 20:60-2, 3/73;
     46+, 4/73.
M20 Butler, Scot. "Forest Fable." American Forests 80:
     38-41, 1/74.
M21 Campbell, Jean. "Chickens Used to Be Like People!"
     Farm Journal 95:58, 4/71.
M22 Chemistry. "Dr. Hokzter, the Alchemist." Chemistry
     46:3, 4/73.
M23 _____. "Pollution Solutions on Cloud Nine." Chem-
     istry 46:4, 10/73.
M24 _____. "Solving One Problem Nearly Always Leads
     to Another." Chemistry 42:5, 4/69.
M25 Cheney, Margaret. "Bird Is a Verb." Audubon 72:
     42-3, 1/70.
M26 Ciardi, John. "Migrations and Madness; Mallards."
     Saturday Review 55:9, 5/6/72.
M27 Coffman, Bob. "Great Rain Scandal." Farm Journal
     97:40, 1/73.
M28 Cole, Dollie Ann McVey. "Old Gray Mare Ain't What
     You Think." Saturday Evening Post 246:64-7, 4/74.
M29 Cole, Henry S. "Environmental Degradation Preserve."
     Science and Public Affairs 30:53-5, 9/74.
M30 Datamation. "April Foolishness." Datamation 17:22-
     35, 4/1/71; 18:50-3, 4/72; 19:68-73, 4/73; 20:112-
     15+, 4/74.
M31 Davis, Carl. "As Junior Scientists See It." Catholic
     School Journal 69:16-17, 12/69.
M32 Deford, Frank. "Desecrate with Howls So Jolly."
     Sports Illustrated 31:48-50, 12/15/69.
M33 Dempewolff, Richard F. "You Got to Get Used to
     Harry; Building a Cabin, Pennsylvania's Pocono
     Mountains." American Forests 75:20-3+, 5/69.
M34 Dobbs, Kildare. "Dissertation on the Beaver"; excerpts
     from The Great Fur Opera. Natural History 80:8+,
     6/71.
M35 Dunn, Harold. "Young Scientists Tackle Mysteries of
     the Deep." Science Digest 71:66-8, 6/72.
M36 Dunne, D. Michael. "It's a Breed, It's a Strain, It's
     Superchicken!" Farm Journal 95:19, 11/71.
M37 Ebel, Fred. "Ham and the Lady Psychologist."

Popular Electronics 33:60-1+, 9/70.

M38 Ecclesine, Joe. "Measure for Measure." Saturday
Review 55:75, 8/19/72.

M39 Ellis, H. F. "Naked-Ape Crisis." New Yorker 44:
129-31, 3/23/68.

M40 Environment. "North Pole Papers: an Environment
Exclusive." Environment 15:2-3+, 12/73.

M41 _____. "Pollution Can Be Fun." Environment 16:
12-19, 4/74.

M42 Esquire. "Thanks a Lot." Esquire 74:58-9, 7/70.

M43 Farm Journal. "Smartweed: Grass with a Ph.D."
Farm Journal 97:4, 6/73.

M44 Flying. "Say Again Please." Flying 84:82-3, 3/69.

M45 Ford, Corey. "Cousin Ewen's Elk Call." Field &
Stream 73:6+, 9/68.

M46 _____. "Uncle Perk's Bee Tree." Field & Stream
74:8+, 8/69.

M47 Ford, Glenn and Redfield, Margaret. "Glenn Ford,
Star Gardener"; excerpts from Glenn Ford, RFD
Beverly Hills. American Home 73:24+, 4/70.

M48 Fosarelli, Pat. "One Life to Lead-82." Chemistry
45:29, 4/72.

M49 Garson, Barbara. "Who Needs It? Harper's 249:6-7,
9/74.

M50 Gibson, Henry. "Memo: Futuristic Antipollution Musical." Audubon 72:144-5, 9/70.

M51 Gillham, Charles E. "Tomorrow's Critters." Audo-
bon 72:41-3, 11/70.

M52 Gittelson, Natalie. "Up the Laboratory." Harper's
Bazaar 102:16-17+, 6/70.

M53 Greenberg, D. S. "Atlantic Community: G. Swinger
Takes Part in Discussions." Science 166:852-3,
11/14/69.

M54 Hamburger, Philip. "Double Bollix." New Yorker 44:
24-6, 6/22/68.

M55 Harnett, Ellen. "How to Behave at a Nursery."
House Beautiful 113:28-9, 6/71.

M56 _____. "Who Moved that Tree?" House Beautiful
111:15+, 4/69.

M57 Harvey, Mae Eure. "This Mad, Mad Modern Math."
Kentucky School Journal 47:13+, 11/68.

M58 Harvey, Ronald G. "Migratory Habits of the Scientific
Goose." Science 163:764-5, 2/21/69.

M59 Hayne, Arnold. "Carry On, Singh." Look 32:82,
4/16/68.

M60 Hellman, Lillian. "Turtle"; excerpt from Pentimento.
Esquire 79:146-9+, 6/73.

M61 Hills, L. Rust. "To Fix or Not to Fix the TV Pic-
     ture"; excerpt from How to Do Things Right.
     Reader's Digest 101:119-20, 11/72.
M62 Ho, Rita. "Ion-Exchange Fable." Chemistry 44:26,
     9/71.
M63 Hollifield, John H. "Tell Me that You Love Me, Junie
     Computer." Educational Technology 14:42-3, 1/74.
M64 Howard, Jane. Parting Shots: "The Diary of a Pol-
     luter." Life 70:71-2, 4/23/71.
M65 Jacobson, Pete. "Elements of a Short Story." Chem-
     istry 41:36, 11/68.
M66 Jensen, William B. "Chemist's Annotated Mother Goose
     of Modern Bonding Theory." Chemistry 45:13-5,
     6/72.
M67 Jones, C. Dalton. "Pocket Math." National Elemen-
     tary Principal 53:56-7, 1/74.
M68 Karrer, Paul. "Rotating and Resolving"; a Tragicomic
     Popular Play, tr. by G. B. Kauffman and H. K. Dos-
     wald. Chemistry 47:8-12, 4/74.
M69 Keefauver, John D. "Henry Littlefinger and the Great
     Three-Month Smog Escape." National Review 20:
     1220-1, 12/3/68.
M70 Keillor, Garrison. "Re: the Tower Project." New
     Yorker 47:25, 8/28/71.
M71 Kohler, Carl. "Live Wire with a Loot Locator."
     Popular Electronics 30:45-9, 6/69.
M72 Kurz, R. C. "Long Live the Data Administrator."
     Datamation 19:72-4, 3/73.
M73 Lamm, Heinrich. "The Metric System." Journal of
     the American Medical Association 218:257-8,
     10/11/71.
M74 Lander, Lee. "Why Porpoises Grin." Motor Boating
     and Sailing 130:90, 12/72.
M75 Lemons, Wayne. "Technician Who Knew Too Much."
     Radio-Electronics 39:68-9, 2/68.
M76 Lesser, M. L. "Use of a Validated Numerical Model
     for Forecasting." Datamation 17:34, 4/1/71.
M77 Levine, F. S. "Troubled Romance of Little Mary Mass
     and Speedy Edward Energy." Chemistry 44:32,
     5/71.
M78 Lifton, Robert Jay. "Birdbrains"; excerpt from Birds.
     Atlantic Monthly 224:46-7, 8/69.
M79 Lindley, Pete. "Field Application Note Identification
     of Right and Left Hand." Datamation 17:35, 4/1/71.
M80 Logsdon, Gene. "Cows Are Out!" Farm Journal 93:
     36, 11/69.
M81 _____. "Cure a Kicking Cow? Shoot Her!" Farm

Journal 92:81, 4/68.

M82 _____. "Why Aren't You Farming?" Farm Journal
93:64B-64C, 4/69.

M83 Loshem, D. Neil. "Naked Came the Time-Sharer."
Datamation 17:28-30, 4/1/71.

M84 Ludwig, Jack. "Town Mouse and the Country Mouse."
Datamation 17:31, 4/1/71.

M85 McCall, Bruce. "Widget: Man's Ingenious Ally."
Harper's 247:12, 12/73.

M86 McCormick, Gina. "Won't You Come to Tea?"
McCall's 95:34+, 3/68.

M87 McDowell, Charles, Jr. "Better Living with Machin-
ery"; excerpt from What Did You Have in Mind?
Reader's Digest 97:113-14, 8/70.

M88 Meyer, Alfred. "Animal Kingdom Ball." Natural History 78:10+, 4/69.

M89 Miller, Dennis. "Game Preserves." Saturday Review
55:67, 8/5/72.

M90 Morgenstern, Joseph. "Radicalization of an Eater."
Newsweek 77:11, 1/18/71.

M91 Morrison, Peter A. "Interdisciplinary Obfuscation";
excerpt from address. Saturday Review Science 1:
15, 4/73.

M92 Mudge, Marguerite. "Travel for the Birds." Holiday
53:24-5, 3/73.

M93 Mulhern, Thomas P. "Witch Doctor's System." Journal of Systems Management 22:34-5, 1/71.

M94 Nathan, Simon. "Simon Says: [International Exposition
on the Environment, 1974]." Popular Photography 75:
52+, 9/74.

M95 National Elementary Principal. "Tale of a Chessboard."
National Elementary Principal 53:82-4, 1/74.

M96 Nelson, Brad. "Triumph Goes to the Fair." Farm
Journal 98A4, 8/74.

M97 New Yorker. Notes and Comment: "[Lunar Geology]."
New Yorker 46:25, 6/13/70.

M98 _____. Notes and Comment: "Printed Material as
Compost." New Yorker 46:33, 3/21/70.

M99 Newsweek. "How to Stop Worrying and Love the Computer." Newsweek 76:18, 7/27/70.

M100 Novick, Sheldon. Jaundiced Eye: "[Atomic Power
Plants]." Environment 16:inside cover, 4/74.

M101 _____. Jaundiced Eye: "Brontosaurus Ecology
Limousines." Environment 15:inside cover, 10/73.

M102 _____. Jaundiced Eye: "Controversy over Morpig,
Commercial Aphrodisiac." Environment 15:inside
cover, 9/73.

M103 _____. Jaundiced Eye: "[Noise Control]." Environ
      ment 15:inside cover, 12/73.
M104 _____. Jaundiced Eye: "Nuclear Wastes from
      Atomic Power Plants." Environment 15:inside cover,
      11/73.
M105 _____. Jaundiced Eye: "[Petroleum Supply]." En-
      vironment 15:inside cover, 5/73.
M106 _____. Jaundiced Eye: "Project Plowshare." En-
      vironment 15:inside cover, 7/73.
M107 _____. Jaundiced Eye: "[Stilbestrols]." Environ-
      ment 14:49, 9/72.
M108 Oesper, Ralph E. "Chemical Anecdotes." Chemistry
      46:29, 1/73.
M109 Oldfield, Barney. "How to Succeed in Public Relations
      by Really Trying; Aviation and Space Writing."
      Vital Speeches 40:726-9, 9/15/74.
M110 Organic Gardening and Farming. "Letter from a Little
      Old Lady in Tennis Shoes." Organic Gardening and
      Farming 16:46-8, 9/69.
M111 Pantages, Angeline. "Kids and Computers." Datama-
      tion 16:56-7, 8/1/70.
M112 Park, W. B. "Adam and Eve Ltd.; an Ecological
      Fable." Look 34:67-8, 4/21/70.
M113 Perelman, Sidney Joseph. "Mad about the Girl." Holi-
      day 48:80-1, 9/70.
M114 Peterson, Robert. "Say Again Everything after ATC
      Clears..." Flying 88:62-4, 1/71.
M115 Physics Today. "Resonances." Physics Today 27:73,
      2/74; 73, 5/74; 73, 10/74.
M116 _____. "Visit from Daedalus." Physics Today 21:
      17+, 11/68.
M117 Purcell, Ann. "Do Chickens Lay Nest Eggs?" Harvest
      Years 9:30-2, 8/69.
M118 Putnam, Patrick F. "He's Big! He's Bashful! He
      Smells Bad! Great Skunk Ape of South Florida."
      Sports Illustrated 35:44-6, 8/30/71.
M119 Ramparts. Editorial: [Environmental Movement].
      Ramparts 8:2+, 5/70.
      Redfield, Margaret. SEE: Ford, Glenn.
M120 Rogers, Greg. "More Oceans and Children." Sea
      Front 19:209-10, 7/73.
M121 _____. "Oceans and Children." Sea Front 19:114-
      16, 3/73.
M122 Roiphe, Anne Richardson. "Mad Diary of a Manhattan
      Ecologist." New York Times Magazine p. 6+, 10/
      17/71; reply, N. Barnes, p. 98, 11/7/71.
M123 Rosser, Donald S. "Demise of Mr. X." Education

Digest 34:35, 12/68.

M124 Rosten, Leo. "Romance of Digital Computers"; excerpt from Dear Herm. Saturday Review World 1: 34, 3/9/74.

M125 Sahl, Mort. "Motor Trend Interview." Motor Trend 21:93-8, 12/69.

M126 Sanders, Jacquin. "Beware of Fierce Breeders! Guard Dog Breeders." Sports Illustrated 31:30-2, 11/10/69.

M127 Schramm, Robert W. "Now Everybody Clap Your Hands." Physics Teacher 12:407-10, 10/74.

M128 Science News. "Off the Beat." Science News 105: 110, 144, 214, 308, 326, 342; 106:77, 94, 171, 2/16, 3/2, 3/30, 5/11-25, 8/5-10, 9/14/74.

M129 Server, O. B. "Peripatosis--the Scientific Disease." Physiologist 14:90-4, 5/71.

M130 Shaw, Mary. "360/Curse: Hymn of Hate." Datamation 17:31, 4/1/71.

M131 Sheahen, Thomas P. "Resonances; a Typical Day in Basic Research, Wall Street Style." Physics Today 26:67, 8/73.

M132 Shedley, Ethan I. "Big System Games." Datamation 17:22-5, 4/1/71.

M133 Shoemake, Helen C. "Incident at Jasper: Is Speaking Out of Date?" National Parks 42:15, 3/68.

M134 Simons, Mary. "Report on Troubles in Pandasville: Regent's Park Zoo, London." Look 33:22, 10/21/69.

M135 Stanton, Will. "Old Ecology Try." Reader's Digest 101:161-4, 10/72.

M136 Starnes, Richard. "Anthropomorphizers Are Coming!" Field & Stream 74:22+, 9/69.

M137 Stoddard, John L. "Systems Insights; a Fable." Journal of Systems Management 25:15, 10/74.

M138 Stone, Yvonne. "Bestiary; with Biographical Sketch." Physics Today 21:34-5, 11/68.

M139 Sutheim, Peter E. "Testing with Black Noise." Radio-Electronics 39:72, 4/68.

M140 Teale, Edwin Way. "Windows on Wildlife"; excerpt from A Naturalist Buys an Old Farm. Audubon 76: 50-5, 11/74.

M141 Tomkins, Calvin. "Equus Caballus." New Yorker 45:28-9, 1/24/70.

M142 _____. "How Now?" New Yorker 46:28, 1/23/71.

M143 _____. "Rhinoceros: an Appreciation." New Yorker 47:59-61, 11/20/71.

M144 Tullius, F. P. "Talking to Your Veggies." New Yorker 49:26-7, 8/13/73.

M145 Wade, Nicholas. "Great Race: Virus Find Awakens
       Hope for Sufferers; Wagonband Theory of Nobel-
       genesis." Science 174:1112, 12/10/71.
M146 Waterhouse, Keith. "Shocking Truth about Electricity."
       Reader's Digest 94:108-10, 1/69.
M147 Whitener, Bruce C. "Fale for Our Time." Datama-
       tion 17:52-4, 12/15/71.
M148 Wilkinson, Denys. "Slidemanship." Physics Today
       26:85, 3/73; 71, 5/73.
M149 Willard, Hal. "Newton Didn't Give a Fig." Science
       Teacher 40:65, 4/73.
M150 Williamson, Dereck. "Cement Mixing Made Easy."
       Saturday Review 54:12, 4/17/71.
M151 Wolfle, Dael. "Potomac Valley Test Facility." Sci-
       ence 165:969, 9/5/69; Saturday Review 52:67,
       11/1/69.
M152 Woods, Tom. "Just So Programs." Datamation 17:
       26-7, 4/1/71.
M153 Yates, Brock and Bodine, Lloyd T., eds. "Balloon-
       foot Bodine's Gas Saving Guide"; Interview. Car
       and Driver 19:58-61+, 3/74.
M154 Yohe, G. R. "Zerane and Some Derivatives." Chem-
       istry 46:11-13, 4/73.
M155 Zinsser, William Knowlton. "Electronic Coup de
       Grass." Life 67:10, 8/22/69.
M156 _____. "Mouse in the Mousse." Life 72:24,
       5/26/72.

SOCIAL RELATIONSHIPS

N1   Ace, Goodman. "Land of the Pilgrims' Pride." Saturday Review World 2:28, 11/16/74.

N2   _____. "More Pleased to Get than to Give." Saturday Review 54:6, 1/2/71.

N3   _____. "Where There's a Ding There's a Dong." Saturday Review World 1:10, 10/9/73.

N4   Angell, Roger. "Achievement." New Yorker 47:24-8, 8/21/71.

N5   Armour, Richard. "All-Purpose Title." Saturday Review 55:6, 4/1/72.

N6   _____. "My Backward Youth." Saturday Review 54: 4-5, 8/28/71.

N7   Auerbach, Arnold M. "Seven Ages of Woman." McCall's 95:36-7, 3/68.

N8   Baker, Russell. "Communicate, Dear Romeo." New York Times Magazine p. 6, 4/22/73.

N9   _____. "Have You Heard the True Story of Thanksgiving?" Today's Health 52:27-9, 11/74.

N10   _____. "May Day Commune." New York Times Magazine p. 8, 4/29/73.

N11   _____. "Night John Alden Spoke for Himself." Reader's Digest 93:95-6, 11/68.

N12   _____. "Noble Causes Need Happy Victims." New York Times Magazine p. 6, 8/12/73.

N13   _____. "Slice of Life; How to Carve a Turkey." New York Times Magazine p. 7, 11/24/74.

N14   _____. "What You Always Wanted to Ask about Wine." New York Times Magazine p. 6, 4/28/74.

N15   _____. "Who's in My Soup?" Reader's Digest 92: 45-6, 6/68.

N16   Baum, Robert F. "Report on the Smiling Pool Set." Harper's 247:103-5, 10/73.

N17   Bayer, Ann. Parting Shots: "A Women's Lib Exposé of Male Villainy." Life 69:62A-64, 8/7/70.

N18   Beck, John. "History of Legalized Prostitution, 1984-
      2004." National Review 26:748-9+, 7/5/74.
N19   Bell, Joseph N. "How to Survive Women." Today's
      Health 47:40-3, 1/69.
N20   Benchley, Robert Charles. "In Pursuit of an Old-
      Fashioned Christmas"; excerpt from The Early Worm.
      Today's Health 52:48-51, 12/74.
N21   Bergman, Lewis. "Reading the Tea Leaves: What Will
      Happen in 1970." New York Times Magazine p. 8-
      10+, 12/28/69.
N22   Bolton, Thomas. "Confessions of a Dance-School Drop-
      out." Reader's Digest 104:114-17, 4/74.
N23   Bombeck, Erma. "Hanging Out at the Pool." Good
      Housekeeping 173:36+, 7/71.
N24   _____. "Husbands I'm Glad Aren't Mine." Good
      Housekeeping 169:12+, 11/69.
N25   _____. "Thanksgiving Dinner: the Pilgrim Had It
      Easy." Good Housekeeping 171:34+, 11/70.
N26   Bracken, Peg. "Peg Bracken's 108 Original Sins";
      excerpts from I Didn't Come Here to Argue. Mc-
      Call's 96:74-5+, 9/69.
N27   Brien, Alan. "Give Divorce a Chance." Holiday 44:
      58-9, 10/68.
N28   _____. "Perfect Party, and to Hell with It." Holi-
      day 44:10+, 9/68.
N29   Bryan, J., III. "Quiet, Please, while I Murmur a
      Witticism." Holiday 46:14-15, 9/69.
N30   Cameron, James. "Revolt that Failed." New States-
      man 76:9, 7/5/68.
N31   Cerf, Bennett. "Meeting Some of the Good Apples in
      Life's Barrel." Today's Health 51:41-2+, 1/73.
N32   Cerf, Christopher; Flaherty, Joe; and Okrent, Daniel.
      "Oh, What a Beautiful Evening!" Mademoiselle 68:
      92-3+, 12/68.
N33   Chamberlain, Anne. "Who Says It's More Blessed to
      Give than to Receive? Addicted Gift Giver." Mc-
      Call's 100:58+, 12/72.
N34   Christian Century. "Footnote from History"; excerpt
      from Ford K. Brown's Fathers of the Victorians.
      Christian Century 89:1139, 11/8/72.
N35   _____. "Frank Incense for Christmas." Christian
      Century 85:1635, 12/25/68.
N36   _____. "Gift-Buying Guide." Christian Century 87:
      1499, 12/9/70.
N37   _____. "Mementos for the Moon." Christian Cen-
      tury 86:937, 7/9/69.
N38   _____. Pen-Ultimate: "Flagrant Fragrances."

Christian Century 85:1003, 8/7/68.

N39 _____. "Rags: a Collector's Item?" Christian
Century 85:1611, 12/18/68.

N40 _____. "A Ward Award." Christian Century 87:711,
6/2/70.

N41 Ciardi, John. "Is Anyone There?" Saturday Review
54:27, 11/20/71.

N42 _____. Manner of Speaking: "Cultural Note." Saturday Review 52:10, 1/4/69.

N43 Cockburn, Alexander. "Europe: Scenario of Blood and
Iron." Ramparts 13:16-20, 9/74.

N44 Cole, Dollie Ann McVey. "Way to a Man's Heart Isn't
Always through his Stomach." Saturday Evening
Post 246:28-31, 8/74.

N45 Crewe, Quentin. "Eating and Making Love..." Vogue
158:93-4, 7/71.

N46 Deaton, Jean B. "Misery in a Kiss?" Harvest Years
12:18+, 1/72.

N47 Douglas, J. D. "Recalling 1969." Christianity Today
14:44, 1/16/70.

N48 Duncan, Lois. "Year I Won the Contest." Good
Housekeeping 169:205, 12/69.
Elson, J. T. SEE: Kanfer, Stefan.

N49 Esquire. "Esquire's Dubious Achievement Awards Extra: The Howard Hughes Affair." Esquire 77:149-
58+, 4/72.

N50 _____. "Esquire's Dubious Achievement Awards for
1970." Esquire 75:104-13, 1/71.

N51 _____. "Esquire's Dubious Achievement Awards for
1971." Esquire 77:71-81, 1/72.

N52 _____. "Esquire's Dubious Achievement Awards for
1972." Esquire 79:107-15, 1/73.

N53 _____. "Few Words with the World's Greatest
Chili Maker; Interview." Esquire 81:98-9+, 4/74.

N54 _____. "Few Words with the World's Greatest
Lover." Esquire 77:90-1+, 4/72.

N55 _____. "How to Make Friends with Celebrities."
Esquire 81:89, 5/74.

N56 _____. "United States of Bananas." Esquire 75:97-
103, 4/71.

N57 Ferris, John. "Ad Hoc." Saturday Review 54:89,
9/25/71.

N58 Fischer, John. "Christmas List." Harper's 237:13-
14+, 12/68.

N59 _____. "Where It's At." Harper's 239:14+, 8/69.
Flaherty, Joe. SEE: Cerf, Christopher.

N60 Flieger, Howard. "Hats Off to Joe Blow." U.S. News

and World Report 76:84, 3/4/74.

N61 Ford, Corey. "Prize Beard." Field & Stream 73:8+,
       8/68.

N62 Fugate, Francis L. "Savory Barber Shop." Harvest
       Years 8:14-15, 11/68.

N63 Harper's. "Group Soup." Harper's 247:9, 8/73.

N64 Harper's Bazaar. "Bazaar Awards: Winners, Losers."
       Harper's Bazaar 102:158-9, 12/68.

N65 Hazelton, Nika Standen. "Excuses, and a Journal; De-
       lectations Contest." National Review 24:294, 3/17/
       72.

N66 _____. "Well-Tempered Dinner Guest; Results of
       Competition on Dinner-Table Conversation Starters
       with Uncommunicative Partners." National Review
       22:157, 2/10/70.

N67 Hicks, Granville. "Hung-Up for Definition." Saturday
       Review 51:21-2, 7/27/68.

N68 Hillis, Burton. "Man Next Door." Better Homes and
       Gardens 52:174, 5/74.

N69 Hills, L. Rust. "How to Eat an Ice-Cream Cone."
       New Yorker 44:103-4+, 8/24/68; Reader's Digest
       102:180-3, 5/73.

N70 _____. "How to Retire at Forty." Esquire 70:103-
       5+, 9/68.

N71 Hoppe, Art. "Ben Adam and the Angel." Reader's
       Digest 99:185-6, 8/71.

N72 Hungiville, Maurice. "Brightness Is Beautiful." Na-
       tional Review 26:87, 1/18/74.

N73 Kallen, Lucille. "Sex and the Suburbs; or, Meet Me
       at the A & P." Mademoiselle 69:132-3, 6/69.

N74 Kanfer, Stefan. "Cynic's Gift Catalog"; Time Essay.
       Time 100:70, 12/25/72.

N75 _____ and Elson, J. T., comps. "New American
       Credo." Time 96:43, 9/28/70.

N76 Kaufman, Sue. "New Year's Eve Syndrome." New
       York Times Magazine p. 10-12+, 12/27/70.

N77 Keillor, Garrison. "Sex Tips." New Yorker 47:31,
       8/14/71.

N78 Kempadoo, Manghanita. "Letters of Thanks." Ladies'
       Home Journal 86:58, 12/69.

N79 Lipez, Richard. "Canary Island of the Mind; Con-
       sciousness Lowering." Harper's 247:100, 9/73.

N80 Lord, Shirley. "Conversation about Being in Love."
       Harper's Bazaar 103:60, 5/70.

N81 Maddocks, Melvin. "In Praise of Reticence"; Time
       Essay. Time 96:50, 11/23/70.

N82 Mademoiselle. "All-American Game." Mademoiselle

70:208-9, 4/70.

N83 _____. "Quiz: Are You Ready for Liberation?" Mademoiselle 70:236+, 2/70.

N84 Mano, D. Keith. "Psychodramatics; an Evening at the Jacob L. Moreno Institute, Beacon, New York." National Review 26:762-3, 7/5/74.

N85 McAulay, J. D. "On Unwrapping a Parcel." Clearing House 45:250, 12/70.

N86 McCabe, Gloria. "Left at the Altar." Good Housekeeping 168:66+, 5/69.

N87 McCoy, Keith and Simonds, C. H. "Suggested Pranks, Jokes and Put-Ons for Thirty-Nine Really Fun People." National Review 21:575, 6/17/69.

N88 Meehan, Thomas. "Where Have All the Orange Blossoms Gone? Trend to Far-Out Weddings." Mademoiselle 72:113+, 1/71.

N89 Mehle, Aileen. "Cost of Conducting an Affair." Vogue 155:70-1, 2/15/70.

N90 Murray, John F. "Great Southampton Beach Club Put Down." Harper's Bazaar 105:14+, 7/72.

N91 Natchez, Gladys. "Grandma Visits her Hippies." New York Times Magazine p. 74+, 12/5/71; reply, S. Koren, p. 28, 1/9/72.

N92 National Review. "Here It Comes!" National Review 20:1308-9, 12/31/68.

N93 _____. "Here It Comes." National Review 21:1308, 12/30/69.

N94 _____. "Year that Was." National Review 20:597, 6/18/68.

N95 New Yorker. Notes and Comment: [Women's Liberation]. New Yorker 48:25-6, 4/1/72.

N96 Nyren, Karl. "Spiro and the Rotten Kids; Spiro Keats, Bartender and His Philosophy." Library Journal 95:2403, 7/70.

N97 O'Higgins, Patrick. "What Counts about a Man?" Harper's Bazaar 102:146-7, 12/68.

N98 Pearce, John E. "Derby's Biggest Handicap; the Problems of Uninvited House Guests." Holiday 51:38-41, 3/72.

N99 Pearlman, Lanore. "And How Do You Tie Your Shoes?" Seventeen 32:256-7, 8/73.

N100 Perint, Gladys. "I Declare; an Englishwoman's Christmas List." Harper's Bazaar 104:144, 12/70.

N101 Petersen, Mrs. Reinhold. "My Preview of Old Age." Harvest Years 8:2+, 1/68.

N102 Pfizer, Beryl. "Dream Party Nightmare." Ladies' Home Journal 86:52+, 10/69.

N103 Richardson, Jack. "Lively Commerce." Harper's
       241:82-9, 8/70.
N104 _____. "Requiem for Feldman." Harper's 243:116-
       18, 10/71.
N105 Rickenbacker, William F. "Here It Comes." National
       Review 26:14, 1/4/74.
N106 Ross, Rob. "Man Who Loved a Balloon." Esquire 81:
       146-7+, 4/74.
N107 Rosten, Leo. "Cheer for Great Men." Look 32:10,
       7/9/68.
N108 _____. "Cigar: A Fervent Footnote to History."
       Saturday Review World 1:39, 6/15/74.
N109 _____. "Touch Me, Feel Me, Grunt, Growl, Purr";
       excerpt from People I Have Loved, Known, or Ad-
       mired. Saturday Review 53:12-13, 5/30/70.
N110 Ryan, Patrick. "Early Bird Only Catches the Wrong
       Train." Smithsonian 5:92, 7/74.
N111 Schoenstein, Ralph. "When Delicious Food Can Leave
       a Bad Taste: Dinner Parties." Today's Health 52:
       28-31, 6/74.
N112 Shapiro, Karl. "To Abolish Children." Esquire 69:
       119-21, 4/68.
N113 Sheppard, Eugenia. "Resolved: for 1970." Harper's
       Bazaar 103:114-15, 1/70.
       Simonds, C. H. SEE: McCoy, Keith.
N114 Skow, John. "Breath in the Afternoon; Business
       Lunches." Atlantic Monthly 234:84-7, 11/74.
N115 Smith, H. Allen. "Great Chile Confrontation." Holi-
       day 43:34+, 5/68.
N116 Smith, Liz. "Jackie Papers." Harper's Bazaar 106:
       76-7+, 1/73.
N117 Stackpole, Peter. "Nudes on the Street: Have Your
       Camera Ready." U.S. Camera and Travel 31:18-19,
       9/68.
N118 Stafford, Jean. "My (Ugh!) Sensitivity Training."
       Horizon 12:112, Spring 1970.
N119 Stanton, Will. "Getting Along with a Woman."
       Reader's Digest 101:117-20, 12/72.
N120 _____. "Just Call Me Cupid." Reader's Digest 98:
       91-3, 2/71.
N121 _____. "Never Too Late." Reader's Digest 102:
       142-5, 4/73.
N122 _____. "There's No Mayonnaise in Ireland."
       Reader's Digest 98:153-4+, 5/71.
N123 _____. "This Year It's Going to Be Different!"
       Reader's Digest 94:48-51, 1/69.
N124 Starbird, Kaye. "Caution! Conversation Being De-

molished." Reader's Digest 93:107-10, 12/68.

N125 Stone, Bluejay Abigail. "Thumbing Around"; letter from a sixteen-year-old. Atlantic Monthly 224:90-1, 12/69.

N126 Suzy, pseud. "Love Isn't." Harper's Bazaar 101:176-7, 2/68.

N127 Sweeney, Francis. "Tasteful Proposal: Procuring the Death of Unwanted Elderly at the Age of 70 Years." America 131:384, 12/14/74.

N128 Sypher, Alden H. "At Least It Releases our Hostilities." Nation's Business 56:31-2, 2/68.

N129 Temple, Sarah, pseud. "Confessions of a Postcard Fetishist." Mademoiselle 67:191-4, 10/68.

N130 Tierney, J. D. "It's a Wise Child." National Review 23:704, 6/29/71.

N131 _____. "Women as Feminists." National Review 22:789, 7/28/70.

N132 Time. "More Tidings of Comfort and Joy." Time 104:100-1, 10/7/74.

N133 Townsend, Irving. "How to Spend a Two-Dog Night." Harper's 249:11, 12/74.

N134 Trillin, Calvin. "By and Large, That's America." Life 73:20, 9/8/72.

N135 _____. "Improvisation on a Fashionable Theme." Harper's 245:63-5, 9/72.

N136 Trotta, Geri. "Are You Competing with the Right Sex?" Harper's Bazaar 101:170-1, 4/68.

N137 Trow, George W. S. "Your Friend." Harper's 247:8, 8/73.

N138 Van Buren, Abigail. "Dear Abby: I Want to Get Married Underwater." Ladies' Home Journal 85:83+, 6/68.

N139 Viorst, Judith. "My Philosophy of Life." Redbook 143:80-1, 8/74.

N140 Waugh, Auberon. "Rumbles from Afar; Luncheons and Receptions in England." National Review 26:1238+, 10/25/74.

N141 Whyte, Christine and Whyte, H. M. "The Regulation of pH in the Body and in Society; a Parable of the Proton." Australian and New Zealand Journal of Medicine 2:173-7, 5/72.

N142 Williamson, Dereck. "Country Life." Saturday Review 51:4, 8/31/68.

N143 Wyse, Lois. "What Kind of Man Is He, Anyway?" McCall's 95:77+, 2/68.

N144 Zinsser, William Knowlton. "Ask Flora; the Marriage Clinic." Life 72:48, 4/28/72.

N145 _____. "Humming a Different Tune." <u>Life</u> 66:24B,
        5/9/69.

N146 _____. "Nude Bathing Scene." <u>New York Times
        Magazine</u> p. 4+, 7/2/72.

N147 _____. "Palming Off Those Pesky Shrines." <u>Life</u>
        64:17, 6/21/68.

SPORTS AND RECREATION

O1 Angell, Roger. "Sporting Scene." New Yorker 47:92-
    9, 2/20/71; 73-82, 6/19/71; 138+, 11/6/71.
O2 Armour, Richard. "Hammocking It Up." Saturday Re-
    view 55:71, 7/1/72.
O3 Baker, Russell. "Clearance." New York Times Maga-
    zine p. 6, 6/16/74.
O4 _____. "Everything You Always Wanted to Know
    about Football." Reader's Digest 97:59-60, 10/70.
O5 _____. "Football Widowers." New York Times
    Magazine p. 6, 9/16/73.
O6 _____. "Livin' Ain't Easy." New York Times Mag-
    azine p. 6, 9/8/74.
O7 Battenfield, Billie. "Name of the Game Is Incredible."
    Motor Boating 126:56-7+, 9/70.
O8 Bedard, Patrick. Column. Car and Driver 20:28-9,
    11/74.
O9 Bjorklund, Mark. "No Room at the Park." American
    Forests 79:4-6+, 12/73.
O10 Blount, Roy, Jr. "Knock 'Im Out, Jay-ree!" Sports
    Illustrated 38:74-7+, 4/30/73.
O11 Bombeck, Erma. "Backseat Sounds along Vacation
    Highway." Today's Health 52:50-1, 7/74.
O12 _____. "One Woman's Howling Success with Foot-
    ball's Monday Nights and Saturday Knights." Today's
    Health 49:26-7, 10/71.
O13 _____. "They Call This Camping?" Today's Health
    52:52-3, 7/74.
O14 Bottomley, T. "Take Jorgensen Along; Mythical Char-
    acter Takes Blame for Boating Mishaps." Motor
    Boating 123:162-3, 3/69.
O15 Boyle, Magdalene. "My Tussle with Tees." Harvest
    Years 10:17-18, 7/70.
O16 Bruce, Jeannette. "Himalayan Trick or Treat."
    Sports Illustrated 34:86-8+, 6/7/71.

O17 Buchwald, Art. "Pro-Football Murder Mystery"; ex-
     cerpt from Getting High in Government Circles.
     Reader's Digest 99:78-9, 11/71.
O18 Buechner, Robert D. "Warring of the Green." Parks
     and Recreation 6:57+, 5/71.
O19 Caldwell, Bruce. "Guileless Book of Hot Rod Records."
     Hot Rod 27:48-9, 6/74.
O20 Carter, Robert S. "Trouble Never Comes in Small
     Doses." Motor Boating and Sailing 130:56-7+, 9/72.
O21 Colby, Carroll B. "Live and Learn." Outdoor Life
     142:12+, 8/68.
O22 _____. "Welcome to the Club." Outdoor Life 149:
     24+, 4/72.
O23 Cook, Terry. "On Any Monday; Son of the Bumpercar
     Nationals." Hot Rod 26:62-4, 4/73.
O24 Cooke, Bob. "Plainfield's Phantom Football Team."
     Reader's Digest 105:229-31+, 12/74.
O25 Cosby, Bill. "Bill Cosby on Chicken Football." Look
     33:94, 11/4/69.
O26 _____. "How to Win at Basketball: Cheat." Look
     34:65-7, 1/27/70.
O27 Culbertson, D. H. "Baseball, the Conglomerate Way."
     Dun's 98:81, 11/71.
O28 Davidson, Robert S. "How to Fall In." Outdoor Life
     154:96-7+, 9/74.
O29 Deford, Frank. "Sleeps Six to Eight and Goes Glub,
     Glub, Glub." Sports Illustrated 38:66-72+, 2/12/73.
O30 _____. "Time for All Good Men ... Help Defend
     American Sports Cliches." Sports Illustrated 35:54+,
     11/22/71.
O31 _____, and Frump, Ford, eds. "My Battle for our
     Rightful Place at the Top." Sports Illustrated 29:
     56-8+, 7/22/68.
O32 Dryer, Stan. "Serving Up a New Game of Life."
     Sports Illustrated 34:46-8+, 4/26/71.
O33 Dugald, James. "High Time for Haul-Out; Annals of
     the West Bay Yacht Club." Motor Boating 122:69+,
     11/68.
O34 _____. "Member Maintained; Annals of the West
     Bay Yacht Club." Motor Boating 121:36+, 5/68.
O35 _____. "Sea-Going Out House; Annals of the West
     Bay Yacht Club." Motor Boating 122:59+, 9/68.
O36 Elliott, Charles. "Look Your Bass in the Eye." Out-
     door Life 145:144, 4/70.
O37 Engelmann, R. G. "Saunas Out and In." Saturday Re-
     view 52:6+, 9/13/69.
     Epstein, Joseph. SEE: Graff, Gerald.

O38 Ferril, Thomas Hornsby. "Freud, Football and the
      Marching Virgins." Reader's Digest 105:71-3, 9/74.
O39 Flying. "The Reading Game." Flying 94:75-7, 6/74.
O40 Gilbert, Bil. "Pack Up Your Troubles." Sports Illus-
      trated 37:62-6+, 7/17/72.
O41 Gillham, C. E. "To Pack a Moose." Field & Stream
      74:58-9+, 11/69.
O42 Gold, Victor. "Mr. Libuthnot and the New Baseball."
      National Review 20:907, 9/10/68.
O43 Gourse, Leslie. "Up the Slide; Being the Grueling Ac-
      count of the Ascending Wiles of Sly Sy and Burt the
      Body." Natural History 80:20-2+, 11/71.
O44 Graff, Gerald and Epstein, Joseph. "Rookie's Note-
      book; Preview of the Champion Knicks' New Season."
      New Yorker 49:40-1, 10/22/73.
O45 Green, Steve. "Bumpercar Nationals." Hot Rod 25:
      112-4, 6/72.
O46 Groening, Homer. "One Last Impossible Shot at Fame."
      Sports Illustrated 35:56-8+, 12/6/71.
O47 Grover, Robert C. "My Life and High Times in Har-
      ness." Sports Illustrated 33:36-40, 10/5/70.
O48 Harrison, Jim. "To Each His Own Chills and Thrills."
      Sports Illustrated 36:30-4, 2/7/72.
O49 Hazel, Charles D. "Very Singular Place." Field &
      Stream 77:44-5+, 7/72.
O50 Hochman, Sandra. "Lone Ranger." Harper's Bazaar
      105:50, 4/72.
O51 Hollander, Richard. "Boys Watching Girls Watching
      Games." Seventeen 28:102+, 1/69.
O52 Humphrey, Richard. "Mystery of the Musical Motor."
      Motor Boating and Sailing 128:69+, 9/71.
O53 Jenkins, Dan. "Out There with Slow-Play Fay and
      Play-Slow Flo; Women Pros in Las Vegas." Sports
      Illustrated 35:50-4+, 8/9/71.
O54 Jensen, Oliver. "Weekender's Companion." Horizon
      13:105-12, Summer 1971.
O55 Kanfer, Stefan. "Summer Gamesmanship"; Time Essay.
      Time 100:34-5, 8/28/72.
O56 Kearns, Desmond. "Sven, the Remora." Yachting
      125:61+, 3/69.
O57 Kerouac, Jack. "In the Ring." Atlantic Monthly 221:
      110-11, 3/68.
O58 LePelley, Guernsey. "I've Got Two Bees..." Flying
      91:65+, 10/72.
O59 Life. Parting Shots: "Fantasy for Football Fans";
      with Drawings by J. Davis. Life 70:62A-64, 1/22/
      71.

O60   Lindeman, Bard.   "Let Your Son Play Football!"   To-
      day's Health 50:68-71, 9/72.

O61   Mannix, Daniel.   "For Use on Giants, Not Turkeys."
      Sports Illustrated 34:44-6+, 6/14/71.

O62   Martenhoff, Jim.   "They're a Bunch of Corks!"   Yacht-
      ing 126:66-7+, 11/69.

O63   McCall, Bruce.   "Fools o' the Flats."   Hot Rod 26:85-
      7, 7/73.

O64   _____.   "Hot Rod Visits the Luther U. Runciman Jr.
      Collection of Cars from the Golden Anodized Brushed
      Aluminum Age."   Hot Rod 26:53-5, 3/73.

O65   McDermott, John R.   "Order in the Ball Park!"   Life
      66:83-4, 3/7/69.

O66   McManus, Patrick F.   "Backyard Safari."   Field &
      Stream 76:60-1+, 6/71.

O67   _____.   "Big Trip."   Field & Stream 76:64-5+,
      10/71.

O68   _____.   "Dog for All Seasons."   Field & Stream 75:
      50-1+, 8/70.

O69   _____.   "Great Cow Plot: Chase the Fisherman."
      Field & Stream 74:76-7+, 5/69.

O70   _____.   "Mountain Man."   Field & Stream 77:64-5+,
      11/72.

O71   _____.   "Rendezvous."   Field & Stream 74:48-9+,
      12/69.

O72   _____.   "Secret Athlete."   Field & Stream 77:60-1+,
      5/72.

O73   _____.   "Two-Wheeled ATV."   Field & Stream 76:
      60-1+, 3/72.

O74   Mull, Walter V.   "Framed!"   Flying 89:73-9+, 11/71.

O75   Newsweek.   "There's a Straight Man Born Every Min-
      ute."   Newsweek 79:48, 4/10/72.

O76   Nord, Peter.   "Everything You Wanted to Know about
      Ping-Pong."   Holiday 53:33+, 1/73.

O77   O'Donnell, Richard W.   "Swimmer-Training Institu-
      tions."   Today's Education 61:54-5, 1/72.

O78   O'Neill, Jeanne Lamb.   "You've Gotta Be a Football
      Heroine."   American Home 72:110+, 11/69.

O79   Ottum, Bob.   "Boog! The Big Baseball Musical"; with
      editorial comment.   Sports Illustrated 35:4, 50-4+,
      7/19/71.

O80   Packard, George V.   "Bottoms Up to the Bottom-Fish-
      ing Hustle."   Sports Illustrated 37:62-6+, 7/10/72.

O81   Plimpton, George.   "Alex Karras Golf Classic."
      Harper's 242:60-5, 5/71.

O82   _____.   "And the Curious Facts about Another 'the
      Game'; 1970 Harvard-Yale Thriller."   Sports Illus-

trated 35:40-2+, 11/22/71.

O83 _____. "In the Mind's Eye; Competing at Wimbledon." Sports Illustrated 35:50-2+, 7/5/71.

O84 Poltroon, Milford. "Manly Art of Fishboxing." Esquire 82:167-9, 10/74.

O85 Schoenfield, Berni. "Dad, Can I Have the Boat Tonight? Four Teenagers Cruise to their High School Prom." Motor Boating 123:72-3, 6/69.

O86 Schoenstein, Ralph. "Won't You Be Sorry When Camp Helps Your Child Realize his Potential?" Today's Health 51:54-6, 8/73.

O87 Slate, John H. "So You're Going to Build an Ocean Liner." Motor Boating and Sailing 127:55+, 2/71.

O88 Slate, Mary Ellen. "101 Hints for Cruising Guests." Motor Boating 125:123+, 3/70.

O89 Stevenson, James. "Short History of the Spitball." New Yorker 49:36-7, 9/10/73.

O90 Tornabene, Lyn. "Day Arnold Palmer Tried, and Tried, to Teach Me Golf." Ladies' Home Journal 89:68+, 11/72.

O91 Trueblood, Ted, pseud. "Great Days on the Desert; Eastern Oregon and Southern Idaho." Field & Stream 74:39-40+, 11/69.

O92 Tytus, Betty K. "For the Love of Grace." Motor Boating 123:80-1+, 3/69.

O93 Updike, John. "First Lunar Invitational." New Yorker 47:35-6, 2/27/71.

O94 Van Volkenburg, Donald R. "Tin Boats of Scrog Lake." Motor Boating 126:52-5+, 12/70.

O95 Waldron, Eli. "Bobby Shaftoe." New Yorker 48:33, 7/8/72.

O96 Willig, John. "If It Was Six No-Trump Doubled, That Must Have Been Martinique." New York Times Magazine p. 34-5+, 4/9/72.

O97 Wilson, Lee. "Fast Pitch for a Faster Game: Three-Set Baseball?" Sports Illustrated 28:54-8, 5/13/68.

O98 Woodley, Richard. "On My Honor, I Am Middle-Aged." Esquire 76:118+, 12/71.

O99 Zern, Ed. "How to Win at Trap-Shooting." Field & Stream 74:172+, 9/69.

O100 Zinsser, William Knowlton. "Letter from the Golf Committee." Life 70:13, 6/11/71.

SPECIFIC-SUBJECT INDEX

brolgas D176
brownstone houses J40
Buchwald, Art F88, F110
building M33, M70
bureaucracy B25, C18, K77
burglary protection G56
burials B76
bus travel J19
business cycles B39
business education B85, C36,
   C197
business entertaining N114
business management and organization B17, B18, B39, B96,
   B107

cabins--construction M33
calculators M67
Caldecott medal F53, F54
Cambodian Vietnamese conflict--
   American participation K134
camp sites, facilities, etc. O3,
   O9
campaign funds K1, K89
campers and coaches, truck E30
camping O13, O21, O22, O40,
   O66
camps O86
Carnegie Libraries H33
carving (meat, etc.) N13
casting (sport) O31
castles J49
cataloging H17, H46, H73, H89,
   H110
catalogs, commercial B91
cats D127, E63
celebrities F66, I51, I60, I62,
   I92, N55, N87, N102
cells (biochemistry) D104
censorship F16, F80, F112,
   G25, H65, H66
centers for the performing arts
   I44
chaplains L29
character analysis C47
character tests D116
characters in literature F42,
   F82
charities N34
checks and checking accounts
   B22, B115
cheerleading C133

chemical pest control D79
chemicals M16, M65, M68
chemistry M15, M48, M62, M66,
   M108, M154
chemistry experiments M12
chemistry in literature F136
chess M95
chess players O95
Chicago Public Library H14
chickens M21, M36, M117
childbirth D148, E61
children C5, C6, C58, C64, C69,
   C72, C103, C105, C145, C163,
   C169, C192, D201, E19, E24,
   E42, E49, E60, F10, H7, H67,
   H113, K35, M120, M121, I135,
   M111, N69, O86
children's books F53, F54, F55
children's gardens E36
children's library service H77
children's parties E8
China (People's Republic)--Air
   Force K104
Chinese L45, F21
Chinese leaders K34
Chinese opera I90
Christianity L8, L70
Christianity and other religions
   L62
Christmas A34, C60, D101, E38,
   E49, E55, H102, N20, N35,
   N58
Christmas carols E37
Christmas gifts B66, B94, E12,
   E51, F126, N33, N36, N74,
   N78, N85, N100
church advertising L33
church architecture A9
church attendance L35
church committees L56
church music I37, I66, I68, I83,
   L36
church organists I6, I146, I73
church services L16, L17, L25
cigars N108
circuses I7
cities and towns--growth N16
city planners A8
city planning A13, A20, A33, A34,
   A39
civilization--preservation and records N37
classical music I10

United States. Central Intelligence Agency G22, G77
United States--civilization F7, F114, N56, N59
United States. Congress K23, K83, L29
United States. District Courts G65
United States--economic conditions and policy B68, B69, B95, K117
United States. Executive Office of the President K41
United States. Federal Bureau of Investigation G41, G54
United States. Food and Drug Administration M156
United States--foreign relations K67, K84, K112, K136, K147
United States--intellectual life N42
United States. National Park Service J14
United States--politics and government G45, K1, K17, K21, K24, K27, K28, K38, K43, K46, K50, K69, K94, K103, K105, K109, K115, K119, K123, K124, K125, K127, K138, K142, K148, K150
United States--popular culture N128
United States. State Department K44
upper classes F81

vacation houses B118, J17
vacations B20, E16, E22, J53, J64, O6, O11
Valentines N120
vandalism G6
vegetable gardening M144
vehicles O54
vending machines M87
veterinary science D31
Vienna I105, I134
Vietnamese War, 1957 F34, K45, K47, K48, K98, K107, K108, K111, K151
violence in television F13
violins and violinists I23, I67, I74, I75, I87, I137

violoncello I77
visual delusions D173
voting K129, K145
voucher plan in education C14

wage-price policy B82, B116
war F34, K13, K14, K15, K31, K45, K47, K48, K56, K59, K73, K97, K98, K107, K108, K111, K121, K124, K134, K142, K151
war and religion L11, L15
Warren, Earl G71
Washington, D.C.--social life and customs J25, J39
waste disposal M2, M104
Watergate case G1, G4, G7, G8, G9, G21, G40, G43, G47, G55, G59, G66, G70, G72, G73, G76, G79
weapons K22
weather B20, M8, M18, M27
weddings F86, N86, N88
weeds M7
weights and measures M38, M73
whales M5
White House K30, K36, K61, K72, L17
wigs D36
wildlife M140
wind instruments I112
wine N14
wives B74, E6, E9, E43, E46, E57
women D159, F29, N3, N7, N19, N23, N119, N136, N141
women as athletes O50
women as golfers O53
women as musicians I101
women as stockholers B79
women as travelers J2, J47
women in agriculture B64
women in boating O7
women in drama F105
women's liberation movement B47, F44, K54, N5, N17, N83, N95, N96, N131
woodworking E27
words SEE: language
World Trade Center A42
worry D29
wrestling O57
Wyoming--fishing O48

yacht clubs O33, O34, O35
yoga L54
youth D5, D198, I47, L34, N112,
   N125

zoological gardens M134

AUTHOR SECTION

AUTHOR INDEX

Chamberlain, Anne (cont.)
  U.S. State Department K44
Chamberlain, John - dropouts
  C35
Chandler, W. Porter III, pseud.-
  business education C36
Changing Times - middle age
  D47
Chapman, Graham - physicians
  D48
Chay, Marie - opera I25
Chemistry
  alchemy M22
  growth (plants) M24
  pollution control M23
Cheney, Margaret - bird study
  M25
Chichester, Francis - stress
  (physiology) D49
Choppen, Edward
  music education I27
  operagoers I26
Christ, John Michael - library
  publicity H21
Christian Century
  charities N34
  Christmas gifts N36
  church attendance L35
  church services L16, L17,
  L25
  civilization N37
  clergy L24, L26, L31
  collectors and collecting N39
  creation L18
  death L19
  ecumenical movement L20,
  L22
  fund raising B32
  hymns L36
  incense N35
  law enforcement G24
  neologisms F33
  perfumery N38
  postal censorship G25
  presidential campaigns K46
  public opinion polls F32
  quotations L28
  racism G23
  religious advertising L23,
  L33
  rewards, prizes, etc. N40
  saints L37
  stewardship, Christian L30

Sunday schools L27
tape recordings F31
theology L21
transplantation of organs, tis-
  sues, etc. L32
U.S. Congress chaplains L29
Vietnamese War F34, K45, K47,
  K48
war and religion L15
youth and religion L34
Chute, B. J. - authorship F35
Ciardi, John
  aviation laws and regulations
  G26
  books--reprints F36
  courage D50
  ducks M26
  interstellar communication N41
  Italians J13
  political ethics K49
  U.S. intellectual life N42
  U.S. National Park Service J14
  U.S. --politics and government
  K50
Clapham, R. C. - city planners
  A8
Clark, John R.
  college professors and instruc-
  tors C38
  higher education C37
Clark, Sharon - drama C39
Clark, Victor - administration of
  schools C40
Clements, Clyde C., Jr. -
  teachers C41
Cobb, Irvin Shrewsbury - surgery
  D51
Cochran, Betsy - shopping and
  shoppers B33
Cockburn, Alexander - forecasting
  N43
Coffin, T. Eugene - creation L38
Coffman, Bob - agriculture M27
Cohen, Anthea
  nurses D53
  surgery D52
Cohen, Ronald D. - curriculum de-
  velopment C42
Cohodes, Aaron - school boards
  C43
Colby, Carroll B. - camping O21,
  O22
Cole, Barry - college professors

TITLE SECTION

"A. K. Tolstoi's Parody 'History of the Russian State'." Harkins. K74

A. L. Hot Line: "Late Breaking News from the Good Office of American Libraries." H2

A! L! A! A! L! A! Here We Go! Rah Rah! Rah! Conventions Past." Werkley. H121

"Abandoned Chickens." Johnson. A17

"Abraham Lincoln: Lawyer, Statesman, and Golf Nut." Meehan. K95

"Academic Protocol: from the Grant Swinger Manual." Greenberg. C82

"Acceptance of the Month Club." Bennett. F17

"The Accident." Coleman. D54

"Accountomania Computococcus: the Results of Infection with the Newly Discovered." Dentibus and Ensis. D71

"Achievement." Angell. N4

"Ad Hoc." Ferris. N57

"Adam and Eve Ltd.; an Ecological Fable." Park. M112

"Administering Our State Library Agencies; an Application of Scientific Management Principles to a Pivotal Institution." DuFrane. H32

"Administrative Bulletin 2115-2A6-7935-17XP1204536." McKinnis. C138

"Adult Education: 1984." Ohliger. C150

"Advanced Placement Student Explicates Fleas." Steensma. F124

"Advanced Referencemanship." Hickey. H56

"Adventures in Education at Herbert Hoover High." Allen and Taylor. C4

"Adventures of a Fifty-year-old Graduate Student." Hightower. C91

"Adventures of Roxanne: Notes on a Sensuous Woman." Trillin. F132

"Adventures of Superhawk." Christian Century. L15

"Aerospace Bonus Boys." Elliott and Goulding. B46

"After Death the Judgment." Woodrum. L69

"Afternoon with an Astrologer: a Predictable Visit." Stine. L63

"Air: Sunday." Arlen. F10

"Airline Rate War." Buchwald. J8

"Albert Brooks' Famous School for Comedians." Brooks. F25

"Alex Karras Golf Classic." Plimpton. O81

"The Book of Genesis and Mental Health." Grigg. D100
"Book Selection Committees and Warped Libidos." Powers. H95
"Books for Your Stocking." Steinfels. F126
"Books from the Wood." Ellis. F42
"Booktalk Time." Doiron. H29
"Bottoms Up to the Bottom-Fishing Hustle." Packard. O80
"Boys Watching Girls Watching Games." Hollander. O51
"Breath in the Afternoon; Business Lunches." Skow. N114
"Brightness Is Beautiful." Hungiville. N72
"Bring Back the Stork!" Stanton. C180
"Brinkley-Vanocur-Mudd-Reynolds Conspiracy; Edited by Walter
    Cronkite (as Told to William Gavin)." National Review. F100
"British Aristocrat Turns Developer, Plans New City in Underdevel-
    oped Country." Smart. A39
"British Have a Thing about Computers." Berenyi. M10
"The Brolga Bites Back." Stanley et al. D176
"Brontosaurus Ecology Limousines." Novick. M101
"Brooklyn Bibliodelics; Local Children Interviewed Members of the
    Library Staff." Library Journal. H67
"Brother's Keeper." Bledsoe. L10
"Bs: the Liberation of Olive Oyl." Esquire. F44
" 'Built-In Orderly Organized Knowledge System'." Caplan. C33
"Bumpercar Nationals." Green. O45
"Bunab Model No. 7." Nathan. A24
"Bundling Power." Baker. B8
"Burials; High-Rise Mausoleum." Mano. B76
"Burning Issue." Daugherty. C49
"Business of Poetry in Residence." Cole. C44
"Buster Big-Brain's Revenge." Starnes. K131
"Buying Van Goghs for a Song and Other Stories." Vasari. A44
"By and Large, That's America." Trillin. N134
"By Nurse and Machine." Scott. D169

"A Cabinet for All Reasons." Life. K86
"Caging and Care of Young Octopi; a Bit of Whimsy." Demanche.
    C52
"Calling in the Pros." Colen. E23
"Campaign Trail: Snoopy-for-President Campaign: Why It Can't
    Succeed." Senior Scholastic. K123
"Can You Fix This?" James. C105
"Can You Tap This? a New TV Show, and Other Bright Ideas for
    the F.B.I." Navasky. G54
"CANACONDA?" Moses. H74
"Canary Island of the Mind; Consciousness Lowering." Lipez. N79
"Candid in New York." Kanfer. J29
"Carnegie Libraries." Dunne. H33
" 'Caro Nome': an Opera in Three Acts and Four Dictionaries."
    Stedman and McElroy. I144
"Carry On from Here, Nurse." Nursing Times. D143
"Carry On, Singh." Hayne. M59
"Case Against Gargantuan, Inc." Dible. B42
"Case for Negative Money." Granholm. B56

Column in <u>Car and Driver</u>. Weith. B110
"Come Out and Play." Frances and Smith. E32
"Commencement Address." Zinsser. C216
"Comment: Social Science Fiction: Report from Iron Mountain;
     symposium." <u>Trans-Action</u>. K142
"Commission on Commissions." Gold. K70
"Communicate, Dear Romeo." Baker. N8
"Competency-Based Education and its Enemies." Stevens. C183
"Compiler Pessimization." Abrahams. M1
<u>The Complete Book of Pitfalls</u>, excerpts. Williamson. E68, E69
"Composers as Human Beings; Reminiscences of a Life in Music,"
     Schwerke. I136
"Concert Harmony." Wood. I154
"Confessions of a Camera Nut." Jones. A19
"Confessions of a Church Organist." Baden. I6
"Confessions of a Circuit Rider." Ciardi. G26
"Confessions of a Cold-Cure Collector." Armour. D12
"Confessions of a Dance-School Dropout." Bolton. N22
"Confessions of a Movie Nut." Trahey. F131
"Confessions of a Postcard Fetishist." Temple. N129
"Confessions of a Stockbroker." Brutus. B26
"Confessions of a Trigger-Happy Housewife." Loughmiller. E46
"Confessions of a White Racist." King. L48
"Confessions of an Ex-Harpist." Lamb. I79
"Confessions of the World's Lousiest Spy." Botto. G17
"Confidential, Confidential; Annual Report, Credence State Univer-
     sity." Shields. H107
"Conglomeration of Newt Ogilvy." Baker. B10
"Congress in Crisis; the Proximity Bill." Keillor. K83
"Conservative Chic." Baker. K18
"Content of Tables: Conference Tables, 1969-2169." Ellis. K58
"Continental Drip." DeKay. J16
"Contributions of Edsel Murphy to the Understanding of Educational
     Systems." Kerensky. C111
"Controversy Over Morpig, Commercial Aphrodisiac." Novick.
     M102
"Conversation about Being in Love." Lord. N80
"Conversation Piece." Baker. K19
"Conversation with a Computer; Problems Facing Librarians."
     Vagianos. H119
"Conversational Tidbits for Next Library Cocktail Party." Shields.
     H108
"Convert." Woodrum. L70
"Cook It Up and Dish It Out; Organic Food." Bruce. D42
"Cool Platonism or the Hipster's Heraclitus; an Undated Dialogue."
     Raleigh. A29
"Coolest Man in the Room." Lipez. G43
"Cost of Conducting an Affair." Mehle. N89
"Country Life." Williamson. N142
"Cousin Ewen's Elk Call." Ford. M45
"Coward's Guide for Those Who Seek a Career in Education."
     Hightower. C92
"Cows Are Out!" Logsdon. M80

"Creatio Ex Nihilo." Christian Century. L18
"Crib Sheets for the President." Fernandez. K67
"Crimes You'll Never Read About." Tullius. G74
"Crisis Classifieds; Possible Advertising of Goods and Services During Gasoline Shortage." Cowell and Jeanes. F38
"Crisis Crisis." Baker. B11
"The Crown of Jesus Hymnbook (Out of Print Hymnal of 1864)." Inwood. I68
"Cruise Director on the Titanic; Art Buchwald's Column." Meehan. F88
"Cry Wolf"; letter. Gell. H42
"Cryptic Bulletin from American Interior." Bassett. K32
"Cultivated Killing." Baker. K20
"Cultural Note." Ciardi. N42
"Culture in Middletown." Mano. I90
"Cure a Kicking Cow? Shoot Her!" Logsdon. M81
Curiosities of Medical Experience, excerpts. Millengen. B80
"Cut-Rate President." Ace. K1
"Cynic's Gift Catalog"; Time Essay. Kanfer. N74

"Dad, Can I Have the Boat Tonight? Four Teenagers Cruise to their High School Prom." Schoenfield. O85
"Dame School." Cronk. D65
"Danger! Postman Coming!" National Review. G53
"Dark Counsel at Easter." Woodrum. L71
"Darn Clever, These Chinese." Holiday. L45
"Dateline: Jupiter 2500 Report from Committee Hearings on Interplanetary Morality." Stevens. L62
"Day America Went Bananas; Reaction to Shortages." Schoenstein. B97
"Day Arnold Palmer Tried, and Tried, to Teach Me Golf." Tornabene. O90
"Day in the Life; Believer in All He Reads and Hears." National Review. F101
"Day Mrs. Levinson Spindled the Kindergarteners' IBM Cards." Wilson. C209
"Day My Son Grew a Foot." Johnson. E41
"Day that Revolution Became One of the Three R's." Schoenstein. C172
"Day that Will Live in Infamy; Scandal Spinoffs." Newsweek. G55
"Day the Shrimp Began to Whistle." Houts. C99
"Day They Stole the Agnew." Steinfels. K133
"Dead Is a Four-Letter Word." Brien. D40
"Dear Abby: I Want to Get Married Underwater." Van Buren. N138
"Dear Baby Doctor"; excerpts from Mothers Write Funny Letters to Baby Doctors. Adler. D6
"Dear Baby-Sitter; Last-Minute Instructions." Adler. E1
Dear Herm, excerpt; "Romance of Digital Computers." Rosten. M124
"Dear Readers: Library Eccentrics." Atkinson. H4
"Death, Be Proud." Christian Century. L19

"The Death of Alkan." Macdonald. I89
"Death of the Maitre d'; or, Never End a Word with a Preposition."
    Newman. F106
"Death of the Megaband." YT-1708-A, Martian Culturescout. I155
"Decimalization of Music 1973 (Tongue-in-Cheek Proposal)." Howard.
    I64
"Decline of Humor." Stimson. F128
"The Deep End." Dawson. D69
"Deficit Saving." Ace. B2
"Defilling the Prescription; Plans for New Labeling of Prescription
    Drugs." Ace. D1
"Dehumanization and Subsequent Radicalization of Young Dylan Lazer-
    beeme, Defacer, Graffitist, Aerosol Sloganist and Obscenario
    Writer, Free-Lance and Underground; a Closet Drama in Three
    Grim Acts and Six Grisly Grades." Riemer. C162
"Dehumanizing the School through Curriculum Planning or Who Needs
    Hemlock?" Griffin. C83
"Demise of Mr. X." Rosser. M123
"Demittals, Unlimited." Stees. L59
"Democracy in Music; a Fantasy Set in the Not-Too-Distant Future."
    Starker. I143
"Dental Surgery." Amite. D86
"Dentistry and the Nineteenth Century American Humorists." Foley.
    D86, D87, D88, D89, D90
"Derby's Biggest Handicap; the Problems of Uninvited House Guests."
    Pearce. N98
"Desecrate with Howls So Jolly." Deford. M32
"Devil's Advocate." Newsweek. B85
"Dialogue between an Organist and a Parishioner"; reprinted from
    The Epistle. Journal of Church Music. I73
"Diary of a Polluter." Howard. M64
"Diary of a Sports Widow; a Year-Long Log of TV-Watching by My
    Sports-Addict Husband." Bombeck. F23
"Dick and Jane Revisited; Primer for Non-Reading Inner City Teen-
    agers." Israel. C104
"Dictionary for the Disenchanted." Rosenberg. F114
"Dictionary of Contemporary Delusions." Fitch. F49
"Dieting: Mind Over Platter." Russotto. D162
"Dig It." Kelley. B64
"Dig That Crazy Lamp." Bartholomew. D22
"Dime's Worth of Difference Candidate Profile Analysis Theorem."
    Wheeler. K148
"Dining Aloft: a Dyspeptic View." Fortune. J20
"Disadvantaged Youth." Ferris. I47
"Discovery of an Unpublished Manuscript." Armour. D13
"Discovery of the East Pole." McCall. J38
"Discs that Should Never Have Been Released." Fogel. I48
"Dissertation on the Beaver"; excerpts from The Great Fur Opera.
    Dobbs. M34
"Distant Shaves: Memories of Blades Past." Armour. D14
"Divine Dizziness." Middleton. F92
"Dizzyland of Show and Tell." Moore. C145
"Do Be Careful with Whom You Associate." Atkinson. H5

"Fable for Our Time." Whitener. M147
"Fables." Handelsman. F65
"Fabulous Tales and Mythical Beasts." Allen. L2
"Faculties at Large (the Campus Citizenship Papers)." Clark. C38
"Faculty Assessment and Review." Pearse. D150
"Faculty at War." Longo. C125
"Faculty Status for the Librarians at Arbuthnot." Gore. H45
"Faith Triumphant." Brudnoy. I18
"Faking It." Goldberg. F59
"Fallow Season." Spears. C177
"Fantasy for Football Fans." Life. O59
"Fashion Follies." Bombeck. A4
"Fast Food for Thought." Cotler. B36
"Fast Pitch for a Faster Game: Three-Set Baseball?" Wilson.
    O97
"Father Knows Best; Trip to Europe." Porges. J51
Fathers of the Victorians, excerpt: "Footnote from History."
    Christian Century. N34
"Fathers Only Journals; Public Diaries in Hospital Obstetrical
    Wards." Gillespie. D97
"Fear Fans Out." Varnado. D192
"Fellow Principals, Unite!" Weldy. C206
"Female Oboists." Musser. I101
"Few Words about Breasts." Ephron. D80
"Few Words with the Masked Poet." Esquire. F45
"Few Words with the World's Greatest Chili Maker." Esquire.
    N53
"Few Words with the World's Greatest Lover." Esquire. N54
"Fiddles." Kissel. I75
"Fiddle-itis and its Symptoms." Lyall. I87
"Field Application Note: Identification of Right and Left Hand."
    Lindley M79
"Films." Berger. F20
"Films that Will Offend Nobody." Life. F80
"Final Decline and Total Collapse of the American Avant-Garde."
    Lester. I82
"Final Presentation: Athens in the Year of the Eighty-Second
    Olympiad 447 B.C." Mutrux. A23
"Final Solution to Pollution." Braun. M17
"Finders Keepers." Middlebrook. C140
"Fine Art of Fund-Raising." Christian Century. B32
"Fine Print." Baker. B12
"Fine Theological Points." Christian Century. L21
"Fire." New Yorker. J44
"First Days of Creation of a Medical Paper." Johns. D108
"First Lunar Invitational." Updike. O93
"First Ninety Days." National Review. B82
"First-of-the-Year Horoscope for Teachers." Warren and Hardin.
    C205
"Firstest with the Mostest." New Republic. K105
"Five Editorials." Schutjer. L58
"Five Sleazy Pieces." Eisenberg and Ferrell. L40
"Five Worst Jobs." Buckwalter. B29

"How to Fall In." Davidson. O28
"How to Get Straight A's." Hollifield. C95
"How to Get to Our House." Zinsser. E71
"How to Hold the Violin; Beginner's Trauma." Carlton. I23
"How to Make a Great Getaway." Harper's Bazaar. D103
"How to Make a Million Dollars on Your Vacation; Rain Free In-
    surance." Bernstein. B20
"How to Make Friends with Celebrities." Esquire. N55
"How to Order from This Catalogue." A B Bookman's Weekly. H1
"How to Play the Lagoon." Ruzek. I131
"How to Produce Ineffective CAI Material." Avner. C10
"How to Retire at Forty." Hills. N70
"How to Spend a Two-Dog Night." Townsend. N133
"How to Stop Them after They've Photographed Paris; Sabotaging
    an Evening of Slide Viewing." Bernstein. J5
"How to Stop Worrying and Love the Computer." Newsweek. M99
"How to Succeed in Business Abroad without Really Trying." Mead.
    B78
"How to Succeed in Public Relations by Really Trying; Aviation and
    Space Writing"; Address, July 8, 1974. Oldfield. M109
"How to Succeed on a Committee without Really Thinking." Ramsay
    and Ramsay. L56
How to Survive in Your Native Land, excerpt. Herndon. F69
"How to Survive Women." Bell. N19
"How to Take Off Your Pants While Wearing Chains." Pearce.
    G58
"How to Tell Your Child about Sex." Rosten. E54
"How to Win at Basketball: Cheat." Cosby. O26
"How to Win at Trap-Shooting." Zern. O99
"How to Win Contracts and Influence Directors." Armstrong. I3
"How Well You Look!" Sheppard. D171
"How Wives Drive Husbands Crazy"; excerpt from Penny Candy.
    Kerr. E43
"How's Your Piano? Problems of Tuners with their Clients."
    Hinze. I61
"Hubert Humphrey Sings Old-Time Favorites." Von Dreele. K146
"Hugo Flesch Worst Seller List." Wilson Library Bulletin. F138
"Human Drama in Death and Taxes." Fisher. G34
"Humming a Different Tune." Zinsser. N145
"Hummmming." Ace. D2
"Hummorhoids; the Big Slipcase." Beard. H9
"Humor in the Law Library." Roalfe. G60
"Humor Is No Laughing Matter!" Elson. K59
"A Humorous Note." Goodfriend. I54
"Hung-Up for Definition." Hicks. N67
"Hunting Season." Coleman. D56
"Husbands I'm Glad Aren't Mine." Bombeck. N24

"I Am a Press Photographer, I Am, I Am, I Am." Nathan. F96
"I Declare; an Englishwoman's Christmas List." Perint. N100
I Didn't Come Here to Argue, excerpts. Bracken. N26
"I Dreamt that I Dwelt in Marble Halls." Perelman. J48

excerpts from <u>Sons of the Great Society</u>. Buchwald. D44
"Scion." Ace. K5
"Scram Gets Green Light; Spiro Agnew to Rise at Marshgrass."
   Meehan. K96
"Sea-Going Out House"; Annals of the West Bay Yacht Club. Dugald.
   O35
"The Second Captain (Pictures in <u>Opera News</u>'s Files)." I107
"The Second Note Is Free." Cazden. I24
"Secret Athlete." McManus. O72
"Secret Papers They Didn't Publish; Documents Leaked to <u>National</u>
   <u>Review</u>." F102
"Secret Strategy of Nelson Aldrich Rockefeller, the Shrewdly Con-
   ceived Grand Battle Plan of Richard Milhous Nixon, and the Dia-
   bolically Ostensible Recalcitrance of Ronald B. Reagan." <u>Na-</u>
   <u>tional Review</u>. K103
<u>The Secrets of the Great City</u>, comp. by G. M. Naimark, excerpts.
   Martin. J37
"Seeing America." Baker. K25
"Seek Ye First..." <u>Christian Century</u>. L35
"Self-Soaring Information System." Heinz. H55
"Semantic Drunkenness." Spade. A40
"Semantics and Dental Care." Johnson. F74
"Senator Furbelow Questions a CIA Agent." Varnado. G77
"Sentimental Journey: New York Revisited." Hodes. J26
"September Song." Quinn. C157
"Serpent in the Garden"; a bibliographical essay. Kassan. C109
"Serum Cholesterol--the Etiology of Disease." <u>American Journal of</u>
   <u>Clinical Nutrition</u>. D9
"Serving Up a New Game of Life." Dryer. O32
"Seven Ages of Woman." Auerbach. N7
"Sex and the Energy Crisis." <u>Forbes</u>. B52
"Sex and the Suburbs; or, Meet Me at the A & P." Kallen. N73
"Sex School Dropout." Gardner. C76
"Sex Tips." Keillor. N77
"Sexorcist." Baker. L6
"Shakespeare as TV Critic." Mackin. F83
"Shape of Things to Come? Mechanization in the Printing Industry."
   Simoni. F121
"Sherlock Holmes: the Case of the Strange Erasures." Kanfer.
   G40
"A Shiny New Haldeman, and a ... Letter to Santa Claus." Baker.
   K26
"Shocking Truth about Electricity." Waterhouse. M146
"Short Educational Dictionary." Amis and Conquest. F7
"Short History of the Spitball." Stevenson. O89
"Shorte Note on Long Hair." Armour. D16
"Short Primer of Style." Halliday. B58
"Short Story." <u>Mountain Plains Library Quarterly</u>. H76
"Short Story: the Librarian and the Robbers." Mahy. H70
"Short Story: an Unusual Library Exhibit." Christ. H21
"Shutter Shudders." Williamson. A50
"Sic Transit Gloria Swanson (Hippocrates Has a Lot to Answer For)."
   Smith. D175

"The VIP." Maslin. D131
"Visit from Daedalus." Physics Today. M116
"Visual Welfare State." Ellis. D78
"Vital Signs." Fischer. D84

"Wadhwa Proposal: A Case for Legalized Bribery." Sale and Sorel.
    G64
"Wandering through the British Museum Catalogue." Flanagan.
    H39
"War Games." Blood. L11
"War Games." Christian Century. K48
"Ward Award." Christian Century. N40
"Warring of the Green." Buechner. O18
"Was Melvil Dewey a Whig? Being a Posthumous Account by a No-
    Account." Peele. H91
"Washington Householder Speaks His Mind; Interview." Buchwald.
    B27
"Watch for These Birds." Jenkins. F73
"Waterbury Tales: Poem." Wax. G79
"Watergate Gag." Baker. G9
"Watergate Wit." Time. G70
"Way to a Man's Heart Isn't Always through his Stomach." Cole.
    N44
"We Bathed by Candlelight." Sparks. E59
"We Did It: a Moat, Waterfall and Bridge in My Living Room."
    Ayer. E2
"We Don't Want No Boat Rockers." Reese. C160
"We Interrupt This Way of Life..." Schoenstein. F118
"Weary Dean." Miller. G48
"Weathering the Storm (A Christmas Incident at Hiawatha School)."
    Dovey. C60
"Weekender's Companion." Jensen. O54
"Weightless Ward." Piper. D152
"Welcome Back." Motzkus. C147
"Welcome to My Three-by-Five World." Richardson. H98
"Welcome to the Club." Colby. O22
"Welcome to the Club; Operagoers." Farkas. I45
"Welcome to the Nixon Style." Esquire. K60
"Well, I'll Be Damned!" Rosten. F115
"Well-Tempered Dinner Guest; Results of Competition on Dinner-
    Table Conversation Starters with Uncommunicative Partners."
    Hazelton. N66
"Well Timed Piety." Marty. L52
"We're Rotten, Laura, Rotten to the Core." Baker. E5
"W F E M Papers; Soap Opera Script." Cantwell and Gross.
    F29
"What, Another Legend?" Brickman. I17
"What Can We Do with an Organ Pipe?" Jack. I70
"What Counts about a Man?" O'Higgins. N97
What Did You Have in Mind? excerpt. McDowell. M87
"What Do You Mean, Too Hot?" excerpt from A Bevy of Beasts.
    Durrell. E26

"What Else?" Time. K138
"What Happened When Refractory and Brake Ran Afoul of the U. S. Godwit Lobby; a Fantasy." Zinsser. K154
"What If I'd Had to Carry My Organ? (Amused View of Concert Tours)." Gray. I55
"What in the World!" Ace. K6
"What Is a First Grader?" Sanna. C169
"What Is a Medical Student?" Finlay. D83
"What Is a Teacher?" Fisher. C69
"What John McGraw Said." Rogin. G61
"What Kind of Man Is He, Anyway?" Wyse. N143
"What Nixon Might Have Said; Rewriting his Phoenix Speech." Time. K139
"What Now? The Voice of the Seventies." British Columbia Library Quarterly. H16
"What on Earth Did You Bid on That For?" Fettig. B49
"What Should Parents See?" Robinson. F112
"What This Generation Needs Is a Rousing Chorus of the Woodshed Blues." Domnick. C58
"What to Do with the Bean from a Patient's Ear." Crawshaw. D62
"What Was Ulysses S. Grant's First Name? Presidential Trivia." Faber. K65
"What Would Happen If the Students Got Locked in with All Those Books?" Goldmann. H43
"What You Always Wanted to Ask about Wine." Baker. N14
"What! You're Not Going to Thorshavn?" Smith. J59
"What's All This Fuss about Libraries?" Burgess. H18
"What's the Square Root of Supercolossal?" Middleton. D136
"When (and If) Better Presidents Are Made." McWhirter. K94
"When Delicious Food Can Leave a Bad Taste: Dinner Parties." Schoenstein. N111
"When I'm Put in Charge of Cleaning Up the American Version of the English Language." Rummerfield. F116
"When Kids Write their Congressman." Brooks. K35
"When the Slicks Reviewed the Half-Time Show." Boyd. I15
"Where Are All Those Mad Hatters, Wild and Carefree, of the Past?" Bowers. I14
"Where Are They Now?" Buchwald. B28
"Where Are You, Fr. O'Brien? Where Are You, Fr. Fitzgerald?" Brennan. L13
"Where Are You, Helga Sue?" Time. C191
"Where Are You, Miss Bailiwick?" Phillips. B90
"Where Did the Years All Fly?" Bridges. E19
"Where Have All the Orange Blossoms Gone? Trend to Far-Out Weddings." Meehan. N88
"Where Is This Thing Called Poise?" Richstone. C161
"Where It's At." Fischer. N59
"Where There's a Ding There's a Dong." Ace. N3
"White Cat's Tale." Olendzki. D147
"White House Garage Sale." Esquire. K61
"Whitey's on the Moon Now." Eastlake. K57
"Whither Advertising?" Noonan. B86
"Who Has the Last Laugh?" Mannes. A22